THE
BREACHED
DAM

JOSÉ ANTONIO URETA
and JULIO LOREDO

THE BREACHED DAM

THE *FIDUCIA SUPPLICANS* SURRENDER TO THE HOMOSEXUAL MOVEMENT

TRANSLATED BY JOSÉ A. SCHELINI

THE AMERICAN SOCIETY FOR THE DEFENSE
OF TRADITION, FAMILY AND PROPERTY—TFP
SPRING GROVE, PENN.

First published in Italian as
La Diga Rotta - La resa di Fiducia Supplicans *alla lobby omosessuale*
© 2024 Associazione Tradizione Famiglia Proprietà
Rome

Other TFPs and sister organizations are also publishing this book in
Dutch, English, French, German, Polish, Portuguese, and Spanish.

Printed in the United States of America

Paperback ISBN: 978-1-877905-82-7
Ebook ISBN: 978-1-877905-83-4

Library of Congress Control Number: 2024938885

B120

*To Our Lady of La Salette
in reparation for the grave offenses
to God and the angelic virtue of purity
that made her cry.*

CONTENTS

Foreword

The *Fiducia supplicans* declaration (FS) has caused a stir worldwide, not least because of the confusion it creates. FS provides for the possibility of blessing same-sex couples when, two years earlier (*Responsum 2021*), the Vatican had clearly spoken out against this possibility. The view that FS is consistent with this *Responsum* and the doctrine and tradition on the subject is untenable. FS presents obvious contradictions. The Bible and Tradition are perfectly consistent when it comes to the moral implications of homosexuality. FS breaks with this by offering the possibility of blessing a sinful relationship in God's name. Of course, the fact that this blessing may only last a few minutes and is not given near an altar does not change this truth. There is no basis in Scripture or Tradition for such a blessing.

Cardinal Fernández said the doctrine of marriage remains unchanged. But that is not the question. The question is: Can a priest give his blessing to a union that the Bible considers sinful? This is a rhetorical question. Surely, you are asking God's blessing to heal the brokenness in your life situation, not to perpetuate your disordered situation. One cannot reject God's judgment and moral demands and still appeal to His mercy.

The problem lies mainly in the fact that FS does not address the moral dimension of the relationship. FS refuses to name evil. In this respect, it is in tune with the current zeitgeist: The denial of sin, which is a consequence of the dominant subjectivism and relativism today, and the denial of truth, which, by definition, applies to everyone at all times.

Another problem is that mercy is proclaimed without repentance. Everyone is welcome. *Todos, todos, todos,** everyone, Pope Francis incessantly shouts. Is everyone welcome?

Certainly. But not unconditionally. God makes demands. The entire Bible could be summed up as a call to repentance and a promise of forgiveness. One cannot be separated from the other. Everyone is welcome, but not everyone accepts the invitation. We certainly know the parable of the king who invites everyone to his son's wedding feast. There comes a time when the door is closed. In hell, a different scenario prevails. There, everyone is unconditionally welcomed. The devil's slogan is: *Come as you are.*** You do not have to change. You do not have to ask for forgiveness. You do not have to lift a finger to help others with their needs. Everyone is welcome in hell. *Todos, todos, todos.*

Mercy exists because sin exists. Mercy exists because judgment exists. Mercy exists because hell exists. Where sin is hidden, the essence of mercy is also hidden. The aim of mercy is not to tell others how bad they are but to tell them about the forgiveness of sins. All you have to do is ask sincerely. There are no strings attached. I thank God every day for His infinite mercy. I see so much anger and aggressiveness in our times. People would not be as aggressive and angry if they knew about God's forgiveness. However, asking for forgiveness implies acknowledging sin. This is the key to peace of mind and heart. Nothing works so disastrously as denying evil. Usually, things go from bad to worse.

It seems that FS wants to make peace with secular society, but peace at the expense of morality and truth is the most merciless "peace" imaginable. God loves everyone. He loves all sinners, but He hates your sins. He fervently hopes that you will return to Him, just as He hoped for the Prodigal Son's return. He wants nothing more than for you to share in His love.

For these reasons, I welcome the clarification provided by the timely book *The Breached Dam* by José Antonio Ureta and Julio Loredo. It fully demonstrates how *Fiducia supplicans* is the result of a process prepared by a very well-organized pressure group within the Catholic Church.

+ Rob Mutsaerts

[Ed.: Most Rev. Rob Mutsaerts is the auxiliary bishop of 's-Hertogenbosch in The Netherlands.]

* [Trans.: In Spanish in the bishop's Dutch original.]
** [Trans.: In English in the original.]

INTRODUCTION

Revolutions are like dam breaks. Rather than an unforeseen increase in the volume of contained water, it is the weakening of its restraining structure due to undetected deterioration that causes the sudden opening of breaches through which the liquid mass's tumultuous flow drags away ever-larger portions of the vast engineering work designed to contain it.

Similarly, the gradual progress of revolutionary tendencies and ideas, fueled by unruly human passions, feeds a reservoir of discontent and desires for change. But its volume is contained by traditional convictions, customs, and institutions acting as a dam. However, under the corrosive pressure of new trends, cracks begin to appear in the barrier of resistance, weakening its cultural support base, until a spiritual storm fueled by psychological and ideological factors (sometimes accompanied by a powerful preternatural influence) hits society, causing a burst, a devastating wall of floodwaters, and a subsequent reconfiguration of the religious, cultural, and political landscape.

In Western society, the Catholic Church is the great dam that protects the strongholds not yet conquered by the neo-pagan revolution. Based on the immutable precepts of the Gospel and Natural Law, its moral teachings prevent the paroxysm of unruly passions from producing the field of ruins sought by far-left ideological currents. This is particularly true about the homosexual movement and the transgender ideology, whose demands, if successful, will lead to the dissolution of the family and the erasure of the fundamental moral principles on which any civilization worthy of the name rests.

Unfortunately, however, intellectual corruption and the Sexual Revolution have opened up cracks in the once solid and compact doctrinal dam of Catholic moral theology that are now in the process of becoming massive breaches. All it takes is one storm and the ensuing accumulation of discontent for the torrent of unruly passions to tear down the human structures of the sacred edifice that is still the bulwark of what little remains of Western Christian civilization.

Preliminary Remarks

The authors of this book have no intention to defame or disparage anyone and are not moved by personal hatred against any individual. In intellectually opposing individuals or organizations promoting the homosexual agenda within the Church, their only intent is the defense of Catholic doctrine on chastity and marriage.

As practicing Catholics, they are filled with respect for those who struggle with same-sex attraction and pray for those who fall into homosexual sin out of human weakness. They are conscious of the enormous difference between them and those who present their homosexual lifestyle as a reason for pride and seek to impose its acceptance on the Catholic Church.

While doing everything permitted by Catholic morality and civil law to block their efforts, the authors also pray for the radical activists pushing the homosexual agenda inside the Church and for the ecclesiastical authorities surrendering to them.

* * *

The indiscriminate use of the word *homosexual* and its synonyms has generated much confusion in the public. Many times, it is unclear if it refers to someone with same-sex attraction only or if it refers to someone who practices homosexual acts. This confusion favors the homosexual agenda. We cannot equate people with same-sex attraction who resist it and are chaste with those who engage in homosexual behavior. These are two distinct and essentially different moral realities. Thus, we will use the term homosexual to refer only to those who practice homosexual acts and thereby deserve moral reprobation.

* * *

For documentation purposes, we reference some websites and publications with objectionable content and, therefore, feel obliged to warn the reader.

The great tragedy is that many within the Catholic Church, whose duty is to preserve the integrity of the Faith and morals, are working themselves to turn the dam cracks into breaches. They are doing the opposite of predecessors, who warned of the danger of infiltration and tried to strengthen and waterproof the dike walls with timely documents recalling the Church's traditional teaching.

Among them stands out the *Letter to the Bishops of the Catholic Church on the Pastoral Care of Homosexual Persons*, published in October 1986 by the Congregation for the Doctrine of the Faith, with the signature of its prefect, then-Cardinal Joseph Ratzinger. It complained that in Catholic circles debating the issue of homosexuality, "an overly benign interpretation was given to the homosexual condition itself, some going so far as to call it neutral, or even good" (no. 3).[1] A new exegesis was

---

1. Congregation for the Doctrine of the Faith, "Letter to the Bishops of the Catholic Church on the Pastoral Care of Homosexual Persons" (Oct. 1, 1986), Vatican.va, https://www.vatican.va/roman_curia/congregations/cfaith/documents/rc_con_cfaith_doc_19861001_homosexual-persons_en.html.
[Trans.: In this book, all translations from foreign language source citations are our own.]

proposed claiming, "that Scripture has nothing to say on the subject of homosexuality, or that it somehow tacitly approves of it, or that all of its moral injunctions are so culture-bound that they are no longer applicable to contemporary life" (no. 4).

The document further deplored that "the movement within the Church, which takes the form of pressure groups of various names and sizes, attempts to give the impression that it represents all homosexual persons who are Catholics" (no. 9). In reality, however, it "brings together under the aegis of Catholicism homosexual persons who have no intention of abandoning their homosexual behavior" (no. 9), and "who either ignore the teaching of the Church or seek somehow to undermine it" (no. 9).

The CDF's *Letter* signed by Cardinal Ratzinger described with great clarity the modus operandi of this doctrinal subversion: "One tactic used is to protest that any and all criticism of or reservations about homosexual people, their activity and lifestyle, are simply diverse forms of unjust discrimination" (no. 9). Its final instruction to the bishops was that "all support should be withdrawn from any organizations which seek to undermine the teaching of the Church, which are ambiguous about it, or which neglect it entirely. [Because] such support, or even the semblance of such support, can be gravely misinterpreted" (no. 17).

Unfortunately, the vast majority of bishops in Europe, the Americas, and Australia, regions where homosexuality became widespread in the wake of the Sexual Revolution of the Sixties, failed to comply with these prudent 1986 instructions from the Holy See.

In many countries in this large part of the world, along with the legal recognition of civil unions and homosexual "marriage," pressure groups sprung up outside and inside the Church demanding the full integration of Catholics living publicly in stable relationships with same-sex partners into Church life.

The first step for such gravely immoral unions to achieve full recognition was to find priests who would bless same-sex pairs (pseudo-couples) on special occasions such as Saint Valentine's Day, then to do so in pseudo-liturgical ceremonies after the registration of a civil union or "marriage" in a municipality.

Last December 18, the new Dicastery for the Doctrine of the Faith took a highly symbolic half-step on this long road toward full recognition by publishing the declaration *Fiducia supplicans* bearing the signature of its prefect, Cardinal Víctor Manuel Fernández. This declaration authorizes priests to bless cohabiting, adulterous, and same-sex pairs who request it, as long as this is done "non-ritually."

Although the Vatican insisted that this did not represent a change in doctrine regarding marriage and sexual morality, the mainstream media and public opinion interpreted this permission as the Church's first openness to recognizing same-sex unions. Thus, the "non-ritual" blessings authorized by *Fiducia supplicans* opened a big breach in the dam of Catholic morals and represented a victory for the homosexual movement to the extent that this impression took hold in the minds of the public, especially Catholics.

As Most Rev. Joseph Naumann, archbishop of Kansas City, Kan., states in *The Leaven*, his archdiocesan publication, "Gay rights activists pushed hard in their demands for secular society to grant them marital status. These same activists have also sought from the church the blessing of same-sex unions as an affirmation of the propriety of their sexual activity and as an eventual step to granting marital recognition of their relationships." He reiterated, "Why has there been such a strong reaction to a change that some might consider to be simply semantics? The confusion regarding 'Fiducia Supplicans' was predictable. Gay rights activists within and outside the church have been demanding the church's blessing of same-sex unions as a necessary step to the church ultimately conforming to the culture and embracing same-sex marriages."[2]

Some people might find it exaggerated to link the *Fiducia supplicans* declaration with the homosexual movement either because they were young when Cardinal Joseph Ratzinger's *Letter to the Bishops* triggered considerable media discussion or because they did not follow Church issues closely at the time.

This book is intended to help all who lack this historical perspective understand in a concise and panoramic view how much Cardinal Víctor Manuel Fernández's *Fiducia supplicans* constitutes an unusual Vatican surrender to the pressures of the homosexual movement inside and outside the Church.

Catholics who earnestly hold fast to the teachings of divine Revelation and traditional morality need to be aware of the scope of the clash and for how long it has been going on so they can react with conviction and energy.

First, however, we need to uncover, albeit briefly, the true amplitude of this half-step by *Fiducia supplicans* toward full recognition of homosexuality.

2. Joseph F. Naumann, "'Fiducia Supplicans' Does Not Change Perennial Church Teaching," *The Leaven*, Jan. 12, 2024, https://theleaven.org/fiducia-supplicans-does-not -change-perennial-church-teaching/.

CHAPTER 1

Blessing Homosexual Pairs Is Contrary to Revelation and Tradition

*F*iducia supplicans admits "the possibility of blessings for couples in irregular situations and for couples of the same sex, the form of which should not be fixed ritually by ecclesial authorities to avoid producing confusion with the blessing proper to the Sacrament of Marriage" (no. 31).[3]

As a supposed indicator of this difference, the text explains: "This blessing should never be imparted in concurrence with the ceremonies of a civil union, and not even in connection with them. Nor can it be performed with any clothing, gestures, or words that are proper to a wedding" (no. 39). It must be requested spontaneously "on pilgrimages, at shrines, or even on the street when they meet a priest" (no. 28).

"Irregular Unions" and "Irregular Couples"

First *Amoris laetitia* and now *Fiducia supplicans* use the adjective "irregular" to qualify the union of two individuals who live together in a state of habitual, serious, and public sin: adulterers; cohabiting, domestic, or life partners; concubines; the divorced and civilly "remarried"; homosexuals; and so forth.

In the Church's traditional Magisterium and law, they were defined as "public sinners." However, in the new pastoral approach, such qualification is considered a merciless moral condemnation that risks alienating them further. By euphemistically defining their relationship as merely "irregular," a preventive moral condemnation is avoided while using terms suitable to arouse compassion: They are just wounded, perhaps innocent victims . . .

---

3. Dicastery for the Doctrine of the Faith, Declaration *Fiducia supplicans* on the Pastoral Meaning of Blessings (Dec. 18, 2023), Vatican.va, https://www.vatican.va/roman_curia /congregations/cfaith/documents/rc_ddf_doc_20231218_fiducia-supplicans_en.html.

The use of talismanic words (like "irregular" and "wounded") exploits an understandable feeling of compassion for those living at the margins of society and the Church. In order not to aggravate the psychological suffering of the "irregular couple," any moral judgment is discouraged, as it is considered offensive and harmful. On the contrary, the merciful attitudes of "inclusion" and "accompaniment" are recommended as the only ones capable of rendering effective pastoral care.

In the second phase, the compassionate feeling arouses a progressive identification with and sympathy for the "irregular couple," which makes one forget their moral responsibility. The initial suspension of moral judgment is then reversed. Now, the situation is excused or even justified as if it were insurmountable, while those who persist in rebuking their sinful union are accused of lacking mercy.

A paradigmatic example of this reversal was Cardinal Christoph Schönborn's words during the official presentation of *Amoris laetitia* to the press, at the Vatican, in April 2016. According to him, the distinction that has always been made between morally licit and illicit unions came from an "artificial" focus: "There is often a tendency, perhaps unconscious, to discuss these realities of life on the basis of two separate tracks. On the one hand there are marriages and families that are 'regular,' that correspond to the rules, where everything is 'fine' and 'in order,' and then there are the 'irregular' situations that represent a problem." And he concludes: "My great joy as a result of this document [*Amoris laetitia*] resides in the fact that it coherently overcomes that artificial, superficial, clear division between 'regular' and 'irregular.'"[4]

In his turn, addressing the Secretariat of the Synod, Cardinal Jean-Claude Hollerich, archbishop of Luxembourg, proposed a revolutionary "transition from a pastoral on families

---

4. Zenit staff, "Cardinal Schonborn's Intervention at Presentation of Amoris Laetitia," Zenit.org, Apr. 8, 2016, https://zenit.org/articles/cardinal-schonborns-intervention-at-presentation-of-amoris-laetitia/.

> to a pastoral of love," one that "accompanies people in their love project."[5] It does not matter if the "love project" is virtuous or sinful, or if it leads to Heaven or Hell . . .

It turns out that in March 2021, the Congregation for the Doctrine of the Faith, then headed by Spanish Cardinal Luis Ladaria, had peremptorily condemned such blessings in response to this *dubium* from a bishop: "Does the Church have the power to give the blessing to unions of persons of the same sex?" The *Responsum* emphatically stated, "Negative." "When a blessing is invoked on particular human relationships, in addition to the right intention of those who participate, it is necessary that what is blessed be objectively and positively ordered to receive and express grace, according to the designs of God inscribed in creation, and fully revealed by Christ the Lord."[6]

"For this reason," the *Responsum* concluded, "it is not licit to impart a blessing on relationships, or partnerships, even stable, that involve sexual activity outside of marriage (i.e., outside the indissoluble union of a man and a woman open in itself to the transmission of life), as is the case of the unions between persons of the same sex." It is worth noting that the official press release contains this final paragraph: "The Sovereign Pontiff Francis, at the Audience granted to the undersigned Secretary of this Congregation, was informed and gave his assent to the publication of the abovementioned *Responsum ad dubium*, with the annexed Explanatory Note."

5. "Lussemburgo, per la famiglia serve una nuova 'pastorale dell'amore,'" DifesaPopolo.it, May 13, 2015, https://www.difesapopolo.it/Archivio/Speciali/Il-Sinodo-sulla-famiglia /Lussemburgo-per-la-famiglia-serve-una-nuova-pastorale-dell-amore.

6. Congregation for the Doctrine of the Faith, "Responsum della Congregazione per la Dottrina della Fede ad un dubium circa la benedizione delle unioni di persone dello stesso sesso," Vatican.va, Mar. 15, 2021, https://press.vatican.va/content/salastampa/it/bollettino /pubblico/2021/03/15/0157/00330.html#ing.

How is it possible that, just two and a half years later, the prefect of that same dicastery says precisely the opposite, with Pope Francis's signature?

Four Fallacies to 'Justify' Blessing a Sinful Relationship

While explicitly recognizing that traditional teaching only allows for blessings of "things, places, or circumstances that do not contradict the law or the spirit of the Gospel" (no. 10, citing the *Rituale Romanum*), in *Fiducia supplicans*, Cardinal Fernández uses four fallacious subterfuges to circumvent the previous *Responsum*.

First, he claims that Pope Francis has broadened the theological-pastoral concept of blessing, creating a new category called "pastoral blessing," which, like "liturgical blessings," would not require a "prior moral perfection" of the person requesting it. The fallacy lies in implying that traditional "liturgical blessings" would require such perfection when, in reality, the Church never required it or even the state of grace. For example, at the end of Mass, the priest blesses all those present, some of whom may be in mortal sin. Furthermore, blessings fall into the theological category of sacramentals. All treatises on Moral Theology teach that sacramentals, such as ashes or holy water, can be given even to non-Catholics if they ask for them with a good disposition.

Second, *Fiducia supplicans* claims that blessing cohabiting, adulterous, and homosexual pairs would not be blessing sinful unions because "there is no intention to legitimize anything" (no. 40). The fallacy lies in trying to distinguish the pair from the union when what makes them a pseudo-couple is what unites them—in this case, community of life. This is even clearer in the third fallacy, where their "relationship" is explicitly mentioned.

Third, the document insinuates that what the cohabiting, adulterous, or homosexual pair is asking for is only that the "positive" aspects of their union be blessed. It references individuals who "do not claim a legitimation of their own status, but who beg that all that is true, good, and humanly valid in their lives and their relationships be enriched, healed, and elevated by the presence of the Holy Spirit" (no. 31). Here, the fallacy lies in pretending that, in a relationship that claims to be conjugal, the different aspects of the community of life can be separated into watertight compartments, some positive and others negative. In reality, even what some might consider positive aspects (e.g., affection, fidelity, and mutual support) contribute to maintaining the sinful relationship, hindering conversion, and the dissolution of the sinful union. The more "positive" such aspects appear to be, the more they constitute near occasions of sin, if not the very foundation for the structure of sin ensnaring the two individuals.

The fourth fallacy is trying to separate the Church's pastoral action from her doctrine, as if they obeyed two independent and contradictory logics: "The Church, moreover, must shy away from resting its pastoral praxis on the fixed nature of certain doctrinal or disciplinary schemes" (no. 25). "God's merciful embrace and the Church's motherhood" (no. 19) should take into account that "we are more important to God than all the sins we can commit" (no. 27). This disregard for the evil of sin and its consequences—which can be the eternal fires of hell!—begs the question: Why did Jesus die on the Cross to redeem us? Why did He say to the adulterous woman: "Go, and now sin no more" (John 8:11)?

The last subterfuge is to pretend that priests from whom such "pastoral blessings" are requested would respect the restrictions imposed in their concrete applications. The most flagrant case of disrespect occurred in the diocese of Maldonado, Uruguay, where two well-known television personalities received the blessing of the diocese's vicar general during a party with four hundred guests after celebrating their civil "marriage." This Vatican document's application was all the more scandalous because the details were agreed between the beneficiaries and the local bishop after the latter obtained the apostolic nuncio's consent.[7]

For all these reasons, *Fiducia supplicans* represents a break with the Church's traditional teaching on the Sixth Commandment, the intrinsically sinful nature of any use of the sexual faculties outside marriage, and the scandal that cohabiting, adulterous, and homosexual relationships and unions represent for the faithful and society.

---

7. See Julieta Villar, "Obispo aclara cómo se realizó la bendición a dos personas homosexuales en Uruguay," ACI Prensa, Feb. 22, 2024, https://www.aciprensa.com/noticias/103286 /uruguay-obispo-aclara-como-se-realizo-la-bendicion-de-carlos-perciavalle-y-su-pareja-gay.

CHAPTER 2

Fiducia Supplicans Shocks the *Sensus Fidei* of Cardinals, Bishops, Priests, and Laity While Being Applauded by the Homosexual Movement

The prefect emeritus of the Congregation for the Doctrine of the Faith, Cardinal Gerhard Müller, hastened to publish a note stating that *Fiducia supplicans* was a "doctrinal leap" because "there are no biblical texts or texts of the Fathers and Doctors of the Church or previous documents of the magisterium to support the conclusions of [*Fiducia supplicans*]."

If the Church can add new sacramentals to existing ones, it cannot "change their meaning in such a way as to trivialize sin." "A blessing," the cardinal states, "has an objective reality of its own and thus cannot be redefined at will to fit a subjective intention that is contrary to the nature of a blessing," becoming an *ad hoc* creation "to bless situations that are contrary to the law or spirit of the gospel."

He concludes emphatically, "Blessing a reality that is contrary to creation is not only impossible, it is blasphemy."[8] Indeed, to "say something good" (*benedicere*) about a sinful relationship in God's Name is to take His Holy Name in vain.

Suggestions That "Would Cause Scandal and Incomprehension"

Speaking to Uruguay's largest newspaper, Cardinal Daniel Sturla, archbishop of Montevideo, said, "It is a controversial issue and is dividing waters within the Church." "A priest clearly blesses all

---

8. Gerhard Ludwig Müller, "The Only Blessing of Mother Church Is the Truth That Will Set Us Free—Note on the Declaration *Fiducia supplicans*," in "Müller – 'Fiducia Supplicans' Is 'Self-Contradictory,'" *The Pillar*, Dec. 21, 2023, https://www.pillarcatholic.com/p/muller-fiducia-supplicans-is-self.

people," but "blessing a homosexual couple is something else. It is no longer blessing persons but a couple, and the whole tradition of the Church, including a document issued two years ago, says that it is not possible to do this." He reiterates, "An unmarried couple is also not blessed. Unions that the Church itself says are not in accordance with God's plan cannot be blessed."[9]

For his part, in a Christmas message, Cardinal Robert Sarah, prefect emeritus of the Congregation for Divine Worship, called on bishops' conferences and every bishop to oppose *Fiducia supplicans*. "In so doing, one does not oppose Pope Francis but firmly and radically opposes a heresy seriously undermining the Church, the Body of Christ, because it is contrary to the Catholic Faith and Tradition."[10]

His message echoes the joint statement by Most Rev. Tomasz Peta, archbishop of Astana, Kazakhstan, and his auxiliary bishop, Most Rev. Athanasius Schneider, which states that Cardinal Fernández's document is a "great deception" and that its proposed blessings of same-sex pairs "directly and seriously contradict Divine Revelation and the uninterrupted, bimillennial doctrine and practice of the Catholic Church."[11]

In his turn, the auxiliary bishop of s'Hertogenbosch (The Netherlands), Most Rev. Rob Mutsaerts, wrote on his blog a note with worldwide repercussions, asking, "Can God give his blessing to

---

9. Walter Sánchez Silva, "*Fiducia supplicans* 'no era un tema' para Navidad, asegura Cardenal," ACI Prensa, Dec. 25, 2023, https://www.aciprensa.com/noticias/102489 /cardenal-sturla-declaracion-sobre-bendicion-de-parejas-homosexuales-no-era-tema -de-navidad.

10. Sandro Magister, "'Fiducia supplicans'. Le cardinal Sarah: 'On s'oppose à une hérésie qui mine gravement l'Église,'" Diakonos.be, Jan. 8, 2024, https://www.diakonos.be/fiducia -supplicans-le-cardinal-sarah-on-soppose-a-une-heresie-qui-mine-gravement-leglise/.

11. Diane Montagna, "Archbishop Prohibits Priests From 'Performing any Form of Blessing' of Same-Sex Couples in Response to New Vatican Declaration," *Catholic Herald*, Dec. 19, 2023, https://catholicherald.co.uk/archbishop-prohibits-priests -from-performing-any-form-of-blessing-of-same-sex-couples-in-response-to-new -vatican-declaration/.

sin? Of course not! We love the sinner but hate the sin. The same principle applies to all three forms of blessing (sacramental, formal, and informal). And this is where *Fiducia supplicans* goes wrong: it identifies sin with the sinner."[12]

A few days later, fifteen statements from African bishops' conferences followed, along with a letter from the president of the Symposium of Bishops' Conferences of Africa and Madagascar, Congolese Cardinal Fridolin Ambongo Besungu, archbishop of Kinshasa, refusing to apply the declaration on the African continent. The episcopal conferences of Ukraine (Latin and Greek Catholic), Poland, Hungary, Haiti, the Antilles, and many diocesan bishops took similar stands.

In Brazil, shortly after the document's publication, Bishop Adair José Guimarães announced, "These requests and suggestions of the Sacred Congregation for the Doctrine of the Faith will not be observed in the diocese of Formosa" because, after consultation, its priests and lay leaders considered that "they would cause scandal and incomprehension."[13]

Most bishops and episcopal conferences had not pronounced themselves as of this writing. Only bishops from Germany, Flanders, and Portugal expressed support—a minority of bishops worldwide.[14] Some deplored restrictions imposed by the Vatican document and called for a change in Church doctrine to recognize homosexual unions as good and officially bless them.[15]

---

12. Rob Mutsaerts, "Alweer die duivelse ambiguïteit," Paarse Pepers, Dec. 21, 2023, https://vitaminexp.blogspot.com/2023/12/alweer-die-duivelse-ambiguiteit.html.

13. Natalia Zimbrão, "Dioceses do Brasil divergem sobre autorização da Santa Sé a bênção a uniões do mesmo sexo," ACIDigital, Dec. 26, 2023, https://www.acidigital.com /noticia/57001/dioceses-do-brasil-divergem-sobre-autorizacao-da-santa-se-a-bencao -a-unioes-do-mesmo-sexo.

14. See Robert Shine, "German and Flemish Bishops Warmly Welcome Vatican's Declaration on Blessings," New Ways Ministry, Jan. 9, 2024, https://www.newwaysministry.org/2024/01/09 /german-and-flemish-bishops-warmly-welcome-vaticans-declaration-on-blessings/.

15. See Carlos Esteban, "Obispo alemán espera que Roma deje de considerar la sodomía como pecado grave," Infovaticana.com, Jan. 10, 2024, https://infovaticana.com/2024/01/10

Vatican Declaration Favors
the Homosexual Movement

Predictably, leading homosexual organizations and their most prominent spokespeople applauded Cardinal Fernández's statement.

For example, Mr. Matuba Mahlatjie, Communications and Media Relations Manager at Outright International, a non-governmental organization (NGO) with consultative status at the United Nations, stressed that this is the right direction for the full recognition of homosexual rights. He emphasized that "as a U.N. observer," the Vatican "should use [its declaration] to promote LGBTIQ rights" in the international sphere to counter a narrative that, in his words, "uses religion to criminalize and discriminate against queer individuals."[16]

At the Latin American level, the president of the Chilean organization MOVILH—the leading pressure group behind the 2021 approval of the misnamed "equal marriage" in that country—declared that, despite its limitations, the authorization to bless cohabiting, adulterous, and homosexual pairs "could help to reduce discrimination within the Church itself" and "could contribute to LGBTIQ+ reality in those mostly Catholic countries without civil union for same-sex couples and/or laws protecting sexual orientation or gender identity."[17]

/obispo-aleman-espera-que-roma-deje-de-considerar-la-sodomia-como-pecado-grave/.

16. Outright, "Matuba Mahlatjie Talks to Newsroom Afrika about the Vatican's New Stance on Same-Sex Couples," Outright International, Dec. 19, 2023, https://outright international.org/news-article/matuba-mahlatjie-talks-newsroom-afrika-about-vaticans -new-stance-same-sex-couples.

17. Arak Herrera, "Movilh cuestiona 'bendiciones' a parejas homosexuales: 'Es una nueva e intolerable forma de exclusión,'" T13.ch, Dec. 19, 2023, https://www.t13.cl/noticia/nacional /movilh-cuestiona-bendiciones-parejas-homosexuales-19-12-2023.

CHAPTER 3

The Homosexual Movement's Goal: Subvert the Church With Homoheresy

More than twenty years ago, Paul Varnell, a pioneer of pro-homosexual journalism, wrote in the *Chicago Free Press* that the fundamental controversy "is not discrimination, hate crimes or domestic partnerships" but "the underlying moral condemnation," for "if we convince people that homosexuality is fully moral, then all their inclination to discriminate, engage in gay-bashing or oppose gay marriage disappears." He concluded: "So the gay movement, whether we acknowledge it or not, is not a civil rights movement, not even a sexual liberation movement, but a moral revolution aimed at changing people's view of homosexuality."[18]

Thus, the homosexual movement initially fought to eliminate the offense of sodomy from criminal codes and for the American Psychiatric Association to remove homosexuality from the list of psychiatric disorders in its *Diagnostic and Statistical Manual* (DSM-III), which it did in 1973.

How the Homosexual Movement Got the American Psychiatric Association to Make a Political Decision

In an interview with the *Journal of Gay & Lesbian Psychotherapy*, in its February 2003 issue, Dr. Robert L. Spitzer, the leading proponent of removing homosexuality from the American Psychiatric Association's *Diagnostic and Statistical Manual of Mental Disorders* (DSM-III), gave very enlightening details

---

18. Paul Varnell, "Defending Our Morality," (originally published in *Chicago Free Press*, Aug. 16, 2000), IGFCultureWatch.com, accessed Apr. 18, 2024, https://igfculturewatch.com/2000/08/16/defending-our-morality/.

about the decision's non-scientific and political nature, and the role the homosexual movement played in it.

It all started at a symposium on the treatment of homosexuality promoted by the Association for the Advancement of Behavior Therapy. Its inaugural session was interrupted ten minutes after it began by a protest group of homosexual activists who accused the organizers of "pathologizing" them.[19] Dr. Spitzer talked to one of them, Ron Gold, and told him that he was a member of the APA Task Force on Nomenclature and Statistics, which was responsible for issuing the *Diagnostic Manual.* Gold asked to be heard by that committee.

In their presentation, the activists complained that they suffered discrimination and attacks because the *Manual* included homosexuality. Dr. Spitzer could not remember if the activists stated this clearly, "but implicit was the idea that the only way gays could overcome civil rights discrimination was if psychiatry would acknowledge that homosexuality was not a mental illness."[20]

After the meeting, Dr. Spitzer proposed that the APA organize a symposium on the subject, which took place during the 1973 annual meeting in Hawaii. In light of this symposium, he had numerous contacts with Ron Gold and his colleagues, after which, moved by a feeling of compassion, he began to think about a formula that would give a scientific foundation to his desire to help them. However, he recognized that the formula he proposed was more a result of subjective and political considerations than properly clinical ones: "How much of that was a result of true scientific logic? I would like to think that part of it was that. But certainly a large part of it was just feeling that they were right! That if they were going to be successful in overcoming discrimination, this clearly was something that had to change."[21]

19. See Jack Drescher, "An Interview with Robert L. Spitzer, MD," *Journal of Gay & Lesbian Psychotherapy* 7, no. 3 (Feb. 2003): 101, accessed Apr. 18, 2024, https://www .researchgate.net/profile/Jack-Drescher/publication/244889348_An_interview_with _Robert_L_Spitzer_MD/links/5413bc2f0cf2bb7347db270f/An-interview-with-Robert-L -Spitzer-MD.pdf.

20. Drescher, "An Interview," 101.

21. Drescher, 101–102.

To sidestep the clash between the traditional view that homosexuality was an illness in need of treatment and the argument that it was just normal variation, Dr. Spitzer assumed that psychiatry had never defined what a mental disorder is. Intuitively, one could say that the common denominator of all mental disorders is that those who suffer from one or more of these pathologies are usually unhappy with them. Now, if what the activists said were accepted, namely that there are homosexuals who are not distressed about being homosexual, then it could be argued, "Here's a definition of mental disorder that makes some sense; and based on that, homosexuality should not be in the DSM-II."[22]

In the interview, Dr. Spitzer openly recognized that "part of that was political." He knew that there was little possibility that most APA members would be in favor of totally removing homosexuality from the *Manual*, but many would accept a replacement with the new concept of "sexual orientation disturbance," only "for the homosexual who's dissatisfied" and, therefore, in need of treatment.[23]

This is how the small group of the Committee on Nomenclature, then the Council on Research and Development, the APA Assembly of District Branches, the Reference Committee, and, finally, the Board of Trustees approved dropping homosexuality from the *Manual of Mental Disorders*.

However, that was not enough. Homosexuality had to be accepted by the various religions, particularly Christianity. Since the 1970s, the homosexual movement has set up multiple associations specifically for this purpose. One that is still active today, Soulforce, described its mission twenty years ago as follows:

We believe that religion has become the primary source of false and inflammatory misinformation about lesbian, gay, bisexual, and transgendered people. Fundamentalist Christians teach

22. Drescher, 102.
23. Drescher, 103.

that we are "sick" and "sinful." . . . Most conservative and liberal denominations refuse to marry us or ordain us for ministry. The Roman Catholic Church teaches that our orientation is "objectively disordered" and our acts of intimacy "intrinsically evil." . . . We believe these teachings lead to discrimination, suffering and death. Our goal is to confront and eventually replace these tragic untruths with the truth that we are God's children, too, created, loved, and accepted by God exactly as we are.[24]

It is precisely this *replacement* that is beginning to become a reality in the Catholic Church with the unprecedented authorization for priests to bless cohabiting, adulterous, and homosexual pairs.

A Gradual Decomposition
Process of Seminary Training

However, such a gigantic change in the Catholic Church's doctrine and pastoral care could not have happened overnight. It was prepared, on the one hand, by a stealth invasion of homosexuality in numerous seminaries and novitiates and, on the other hand, by infiltrating Catholic environments in the 1960s with moral relativism and homosexual ideology, giving rise to what was later dubbed "homoheresy."[25]

---

24. Soulforce, "What Is the Primary Goal of Soulforce?" Soulforce.org, accessed Dec. 2003, www.soulforce.org/main/faq.shtml. (Printed 2003 website documentation in TFP archives.)

25. *Homoheresy*—this expression was coined by Fr. Dariusz Oko, Ph.D., in his essay "With the Pope Against the Homoheresy," originally published by *Theologisches* 42, nos. 9/10 (2012): 403–426, where he wrote:

I began my work as a struggle against a deadly, external threat to Christianity, but then gradually discovered that the division is not that simple. The enemy is not only outside the Church, but within it as well, sometimes perfectly camouflaged, like the Trojan Horse. We are dealing not only with the problem of a homoideology and a homolobby outside the Church, but with an analogous problem within it as well, where homoideology takes the form of a homoheresy. . . .

. . . Remembering to 'recognize them by their fruit' (cf. Matthew 7:16), based on the publicly known events of the last quarter of the century, the reaction of the Holy See and the documents it issued, we must clearly, explicitly and resolvedly say: yes, there is a strong homosexual underground in the Church (just like in many other places), which—depending on the degree of involvement of its members, depending on their words and

A direct and well-placed observer—then-Father, later Cardinal Joseph Ratzinger and Pope Benedict XVI—reported on this infiltration. After his papal resignation, when the sexual abuse scandal and the Vatican's involvement in the case of ex-Cardinal Theodore McCarrick emerged, he published an extended study in the Bavarian monthly *Klerusblatt* blaming the abuse crisis in the Church predominantly on the Sexual Revolution and the collapse in seminary formation. He describes how the breakdown in priestly formation reached the absurd point where one bishop, who had been a seminary rector, made seminarians watch pornographic films to render them resistant to conduct contrary to the Faith!

Even worse, "in various seminaries homosexual cliques were established, which acted more or less openly." This moral relativism developed, he states, because until then, moral theology was primarily based on natural law. However, "in the Council's struggle for a new understanding of Revelation, the natural law option was largely abandoned, and a moral theology based entirely on the Bible was demanded." "Consequently, there could no longer be anything that constituted an absolute good, any more than anything fundamentally evil."[26]

---

deeds—may be referred to as homoheresy, homolobby, homoclique or even homomafia. (Dariusz Oko, "With the Pope Against the Homoheresy," Rorate-caeli.blogspot.com, Feb. 16, 2013, https://rorate-caeli.blogspot.com/2013/02/fr-dariusz-okos-major-article -with-pope.html).

Fr. Oko and the editor-in-chief of the German theological journal were condemned by a German court for supposedly "inciting hatred" against homosexuals in an article denouncing the "lavender maffia" inside the Church. Cardinal Gerhard Müller reacted to the court sentence drawing a parallel with the persecution of Polish intellectuals during the time of Poland's occupation by Nazi Germany and praising Fr. Oko's work as "a courageous act that deserves the respect of all decent people." (LifeSiteNews Europe, "Cdl. Müller Speaks Out in Defense of Polish Priest Sued by Germany for 'Hate Speech,'" LifeSiteNews.com, Aug. 19, 2021, https://www.lifesitenews.com/news/cdl -muller-speaks-out-in-defense-of-polish-priest-sued-by-germany-for-hate-speech/).

26. Joseph Ratzinger, "Full Text of Benedict XVI Essay: 'The Church and the Scandal of Sexual Abuse,'" *Catholic News Agency*, Apr. 10, 2019, https://www.catholicnewsagency.com /news/41013/full-text-of-benedict-xvi-essay-the-church-and-the-scandal-of-sexual-abuse.

Without mentioning him directly, the former Benedict XVI pointed to his compatriot and colleague at the University of Tübingen, the Redemptorist Father Bernard Häring, who, with his manual titled *The Law of Christ*, revolutionized moral theology in a personalist sense in the years leading up to the Second Vatican Council.

Chapter 4

A Theological "Fifth Column" Opens Hostilities Against Traditional Teaching

Influenced by this new perspective, in a short space of time, prominent moral theologians went from contesting the encyclical *Humanae vitae*, which banned artificial methods of contraception, to blatantly approving extramarital and homosexual relationships.

Jesuit Fr. John J. McNeill's First Salvo

In the United States, Jesuit Father John J. McNeill opened hostilities against traditional teaching on homosexual relationships in 1970 with three articles in the *Homiletic and Pastoral Review*. Four years later, he wrote the book *The Church and the Homosexual* and battled for two years with his superiors in Rome and the United States until he obtained from his provincial superior the imprimatur for its publication in 1976.[27] In his work, Father McNeill develops three fundamental theses contrary to traditional teaching:

1. "The homosexual condition is according to the will of God. God so created humans that their sexuality is not determined by their biology."

2. "God had a divine purpose in so creating human nature that a certain percentage of human beings are homosexual. . . . endowed with special gifts and a divinely appointed task in the construction of a truly human society."

3. "There is the possibility of morally good homosexual relationships and that the love which unites the partners in such a relationship, rather than alienating them from God,

---

27. See Manuel Rozados Taboada, "La Iglesia y la homosexualidad," *Revista Española de Derecho Canonico* 35, no. 102 (1979): 531–83, https://summa.upsa.es/high.raw?id=0000005260&name=00000001.original.pdf.

can be judged as uniting them more closely with God and as mediating God's presence in our world."[28]

Does God Make Homosexuals?

All authors cited in this chapter assume or accept as an implicit argument the idea that it is God who gives a minority of people their homosexual orientation, which in their case would not be "objectively disordered" as the *Catechism of the Catholic Church* teaches (par. 2358).

This argument is false insofar as it presupposes, at least in the case of homosexuality, that there is no distinction between God—the First Cause of all things—and the second causes that act in the created universe. However, this formulation distorts the Catholic concept of Providence, according to which God is not the direct Author of all physical and moral evil in the world but only allows it for reasons of His divine wisdom that are mysterious to us. Therefore, God's relationship with the evils that affect humanity is in no way positive but only negative. This is true of both the *free* and *non-free* actions of creatures:

> Evil itself, sin, falls *truly and properly* under God's providence since it would not have occurred without His permission and physical assistance. . . .
>
> In regard to the *unfree* actions of creatures, we must speak of Divine Providence in a similar way. Here, too, although God determines and directs them all towards a final harmonious unity, He allows second causes to subsist in their essential and accidental *imperfections*; He does not prevent them from being paralyzed and, in many cases, from failing to reach their ideal (the monsters). This happens not only in the animal and plant orders but also in the human one, and in the latter, not only in the bodily domain but also the psychic realm. . . . Here

---

28. John J. McNeill, *The Church and the Homosexual*, 3rd ed. (Boston: Beacon Press, 1988), 196–98, accessed Apr. 18, 2024, https://archive.org/details/churchhomosexual 00mcne/page/200/mode/2up.

again, we can guess at the *reasons*. Just as God does not wish to interfere with freedom, He does not wish to deprive second causes of their *own action* but, on the contrary, to elevate them to the dignity of *cooperators* (*Summa theologiae*, I, 22, 3). The impairments that may result in the human being are not such as to prevent man from achieving his final end.[29]

Even pro-homosexual strategists Marshall Kirk and Hunter Madsen, in *After the Ball*, their 1989 "gay manifesto," recognize the influence of secondary causes in the development of same-sex attraction: "We argue that, for all practical purposes, gays should be considered to have been *born gay*—even though sexual orientation, for most humans, seems to be the product of a complex interaction between innate predispositions and environmental factors during childhood and early adolescence."[30]

Therefore, Father McNeill argues, one must conclude that the same moral rules apply to homosexual and heterosexual attitudes and behavior, i.e., "any sexual relationship that involves exploitation of another person is immoral." In contrast, "a genuine interpersonal love relationship" expresses "mutuality, fidelity, unselfishness, etc." Moreover, laying down what the nature of an "'ethically responsible homosexual relationship' should be. . . . is a task which necessarily must be reserved to the Christian homosexual community and its own communal discernment of its experience."[31]

The scandal caused by Father McNeill's ideas led the Society of Jesus to ban him from speaking publicly about homosexuality.

---

29. Bernhardt Bartmann, *Précis de théologie dogmatique* (Mulhouse: Ed. Salvator, 1941), 1:287.

30. Marshall Kirk and Hunter Madsen, *Ater the Ball: How America Will Conquer Its Fear & Hatred of Gays in the '90s* (New York: Doubleday, 1989), 184, accessed Apr. 24, 2024, https://archive.org/details/marshall-kirk-hunter-madsen-after-the-ball-how-america-will -conquer-its-fear-hat.

31. McNeill, *The Church and the Homosexual*, 199.

Fr. Charles Curran Enters the Stage

Fr. Charles Curran, professor of theology at the Catholic
University of America (Washington), published in 1971 an
article in *The Thomist: A Speculative Quarterly Review* titled
"Homosexuality and Moral Theology: Methodological and
Substantive Considerations." In it, he proposes an intermediate answer to the question of the morality of homosexual
activity, between the one that considers it immoral (the traditional approach) and that of some modern moralists who
believe that "one should no more deplore homosexuality than
left-handedness," (the neutral approach).[32] This compromise
third approach "recognizes that homosexual acts are wrong
but also acknowledges that homosexual behavior for some
people might not fall under the total condemnation proposed
in the first opinion."[33] It admits, "Homosexuality in every case
is not in accord with the order of creation" but at the same
time recognizes that it is often impossible to change the homosexual condition.[34] So, Father Curran says he "agree[s]
almost totally with the conclusion proposed by [H. Kimball]
Jones."[35] A Methodist minister specializing in pastoral
psychotherapy, Jones explicitly acknowledges "that homosexual behavior in certain circumstances can be morally
acceptable since there is nothing else the person can do."[36]
Accordingly, he says, Christian morals should "recogniz[e] the
validity of mature homosexual relationships, encouraging the
absolute invert to maintain a fidelity to one partner when his

---

32. Charles E. Curran, "Homosexuality and Moral Theology: Methodological and
Substantive Considerations," *The Thomist: A Speculative Quarterly Review* 35, no. 3 (Jul.
1971): 463.

33. Curran, "Homosexuality and Moral Theology," 472.

34. Curran, 472.

35. Curran, 475.

36. Curran, 472.

only other choice would be to lead a promiscuous life filled with guilt and fear."[37] Father Curran wholeheartedly agrees with Jones's assessment: "Therapy, as an attempt to make the homosexual into a heterosexual, does not offer great promise for most homosexuals. Celibacy and sublimation are not always possible or even desirable for the homosexual. There are many somewhat stable homosexual unions which afford their partners some human fulfillment and contentment. Obviously, such unions are better than homosexual promiscuity."[38]

As if prophetically glimpsing *Amoris laetitia*'s controversial chapter 8, Father Curran writes: "In this situation, which reflects the human sinfulness in which all participate in differing ways, the individual homosexual may morally come to the conclusion that a somewhat permanent homosexual union is the best, and sometimes the only, way for him to achieve some humanity."[39]

In his later book *Catholic Moral Theology in Dialogue* (1972), Curran reiterated, "Homosexuality can never become an ideal. Attempts should be made to overcome this condition if possible; however, at times, one may reluctantly accept homosexual unions as the only way in which some people can find a satisfying degree of humanity in their lives."[40]

Fr. André Guindon Also Promotes Stable Homosexual Unions

Fr. André Guindon, professor of ethics and later Dean of the Faculty of Theology at Saint Paul University (Ottawa, 1978–1984), broke more ground with *The Sexual Language: An*

---

37. Curran, 475.

38. Curran, 479.

39. Curran, 479.

40. Charles E. Curran, *Catholic Moral Theology in Dialogue* (Notre Dame, Ind.: Fides Publishers, Inc., 1972), 217, accessed Apr. 24, 2024, https://archive.org/details/catholic moralthe0000curr_c4f9/mode/2up.

Essay in Moral Theology (1976) and later with *The Sexual Creators: An Ethical Proposal for Concerned Christians* (1986).

In these works, Father Guindon develops the idea that sexual activity should be understood as a language since "The body adds sensual mediation to convey affection in a way that oral words alone cannot."[41] However, such language should not follow pre-established moral standards because "sexual meaning is an original human achievement which has to be re-invented, reformulated, and relived by each generation and, to some extent, by each human person."[42] Such language has a sexual fruitfulness that is not limited to procreation because "the essence of the sexual intention . . . seeks the communion of two beings in love"[43] and, therefore, "in certain cases, pre-marital intercourse is probably the better course of action."[44]

In homosexual relationships, "there is certainly a quest for fraternity. This is a positive aspect which homosexuals must develop in their lives."[45] That is why continence "will always remain an exceptional occurrence which is hardly conceivable outside a very special, yogic type of vocation."[46] On the contrary, Father Guindon believes that "most homosexuals act out what is for them the most responsible and the most moral thing to do in settling down with a homosexual partner and so finding a workable adaptation to life." Because "many will find in homosexual friendship the physical, emotional, and spiritual satisfaction needed to live happily and

---

41. André Guindon, *The Sexual Language: An Essay in Moral Theology* (Ottawa: The University of Ottawa Press, 1977), 438, accessed Apr. 24, 2024, https://archive.org /details/sexuallanguagees0000guin/mode/2up.

42. Guindon, *The Sexual Language*, 36.

43. Guindon, 177.

44. Guindon, 438.

45. Guindon, 340.

46. Guindon, 366.

to adapt to social life and so develop all the potentialities of their personality."[47]

Father Guindon's Welcoming of Pederasty

Father Guindon goes so far in his rejection of continence for same-sex attracted individuals that he approves of ephebophilia and even pedophilia. He takes up the defense of an imaginary pederast who is "lonely and starving for affection, [and] dares to put his arms around a child playing nearby or stroke his hair, he is bound to be accused of molestation and rape by a hysterical mother or father." Father Guindon says the parents' reaction bears "the mark of possessive attitudes and of an uncritical stand toward social myths."

"Why, then, are people generally so brutal in their condemnation of pedophiles?" Father Guindon candidly asks. Because "people are generally frightened by both the possible psychological disorder that might result [for the child] from the anxiety-producing experience and by the possible, later homosexual determination of the child's sexual ambivalence." But in his opinion, this only happens "if they have some antecedent emotional disturbances," or when there is "a prolonged series of pedophile contacts." Furthermore, "anal coitus is rather rare – 4%." In comparison "the commonest technique used by pedophiles who proceed beyond mere affective expression is masturbation (45%). The second commonest is fellatio (38%)." But, according to Father Guindon, "these techniques are less liable to have harmful psychological effects than elaborate, reciprocal genital stimulations," and "most recent studies tend to disprove that lasting harm results from the pedophiliac contact itself."

---

47. Guindon, 367.

So, who is to blame for a child's psychological trauma? "The familial panic which is the usual response to the incident." Thus, Father Guindon's logical solution is to cover up the case: "It is the role of the moral counselor in all this to help the family concerned to react humanly and not instinctively to their child's alleged 'molestation.'"[48]

This nauseating text does not come from some sexual liberation mentor or activist like Herbert Marcuse, Wilhelm Reich, or Daniel Cohn-Bendit. It comes from the pen of a filthy professor of ethics at a prestigious Catholic university who was rewarded two years later with an appointment as Dean of the Faculty of Theology! This confirms the former Pope Benedict XVI's accusation, in the article mentioned in the previous chapter, that one should seek the cause of the clergy sexual abuse crisis in this type of writing. Only someone in bad faith can claim that the root of clerical sexual abuse lies in celibacy or the ghost of "clericalism."

A Collective Work Sponsored by the Catholic Theological Society of America

In 1977, a year after Father Guindon's monstrous text was published, the Catholic Theological Society of America commissioned Fr. Anthony Kosnik to direct a joint work on *Human Sexuality: New Directions in American Catholic Thought.*

The authors assume that "the Bible does not provide us with a simple yes or no code of sexual ethics," and its statements must be put into context since they are "historically occasioned and conditioned" by culture and are not exempt from "the influence of taboos."[49] They also criticize Catho-

48. Guindon, 373–74.
49. Anthony Kosnik et al., *Human Sexuality: New Directions in American Catholic Thought* (New York: Paulist Press, 1977), 29–30, accessed Apr. 24, 2024, https://archive.org /details/humansexualityne00kosn.

lic tradition for placing a heavy emphasis "on the objective moral nature of the given act itself," giving to it "a meaning that is absolutely unchangeable." "Thus, masturbation, any premarital sexual pleasure, adultery, fornication, homosexuality, sodomy and bestiality were considered intrinsically evil acts, seriously immoral, and under no circumstances justifiable." However, the authors continue, current studies have revealed "a significant difference in the human value of sexual activity occurring in a context of caring commitment and that same activity occurring in a casual or loveless context."[50]

Based on these premises, the collective work dissents from traditional morality and proposes, in return, "with some degree of moral certitude,"[51] a pastoral guidance based on the idea that "Homosexuals have the same rights to love, intimacy, and relationships as heterosexuals." Thus, "the norms governing the morality of homosexual activity are those that govern all sexual activity, and the norms governing sexual activity are those that govern all human ethical activity." The conclusion is that "Christian sexual morality does not require a dual standard. . . . Homosexuals, like the heterosexual majority, are required to examine and evaluate their behavior in the light of the same values and according to the same moral norms to determine whether or not their actions are indicative of the same characteristics of wholesome human sexuality."

What should be the criteria for evaluating these acts? "Whether or not they are self-liberating, other-enriching, honest, faithful, life-serving, and joyous," avoiding "depersonalization, selfishness, dishonesty, promiscuity, harm to society, and demoralization." In this sense, the traditional pastoral practice has been counterproductive "by advising

---

50. Kosnik et al., *Human Sexuality*, 88.
51. Kosnik, 211.

[homosexuals] against forming intimate or exclusive friendships. Homosexuals living together have been regarded as
living in proximate occasion of sin; they were counseled to
desist or else be denied absolution in the sacrament of pen-
ance. Dissuaded from deep, lasting relationships, homosexuals
who found themselves unable to practice complete continence
were driven to multiply superficial relationships." On the contrary, "a pastor or counselor may recommend close, stable
friendships between homosexuals, not simply as a lesser of
two evils but as a positive good."[52]

Since they deem such unnatural stable relationships good,
Father Kosnik and his team promote a blessing distinct from
the nuptial blessing in a formulation very similar to the *Fiducia
supplicans* declaration: "Since historically marriage has been
understood in terms of a heterosexual union, it seems to us
inappropriate and misleading to describe a stable relationship
between two homosexuals as a 'marriage.' Anything suggesting
a sacramental celebration of marriage, therefore, would also
be inappropriate and misleading. At the same time, prayer,
even communal prayer, for two people striving to live Christian
lives, incarnating the values of fidelity, truth, and love, is not
beyond the pastoral possibilities of a Church whose ritual
tradition includes a rich variety of blessings."

Human Sexuality concludes that cohabiting homosexuals
can receive absolution and the Eucharist: "Christian homosexuals have the same needs and rights to the sacraments as
heterosexuals. . . . An invincible doubt, whether of law or of
fact, permits one to follow a true and solidly probable opinion
in favor of liberty. . . . In the light of all these considerations,
solidly probable opinion can be invoked in favor of permitting

---

52. Kosnik, 214–15.

a homosexual freedom of conscience and free access to the sacraments of reconciliation and the eucharist."[53]

Fr. Robert Nugent and
Sr. Jeannine Gramick: A Troublesome Duo

With their 1975 booklet titled *Homosexual Catholics: A Primer for Discussion*, Fathers Robert Nugent and Thomas Oddo and Sister Jeannine Gramick followed the trail blazed by Fathers McNeill and Curran. Their booklet was dubbed the "gay catechism" as it imitated the Q&A format of the famous *Baltimore Catechism*. In 1980, a revised and enlarged version was released, and the booklet's subtitle changed to *The New Primer*. The booklet's purpose was to serve as a manual for discussion and formation. Or rather deformation, because its answers are notable for their ambiguity, if not denial of traditional teaching on behalf of a more *aggiornata* theology, which "has experienced a shift from an 'act centered' morality to a more 'personalist' morality which gives more emphasis in moral decision making to a person's total moral stance, the circumstances surrounding the action and the effects of the actions on others."[54]

The booklet asks, "Can the Church change its official teaching on homosexuality?" In response, the authors say that the doctrinal development of the Church "includes the establishment of a solidly probable opinion which runs contrary to traditional teaching in non-defined questions," as would have happened in the approach to usury, slavery, and just war. Similarly, the lived experiences of Catholic homosexual persons can prove to be "a valuable contribution to establishing a solidly probable opinion affecting changes in Church

---

53. Kosnik, 215–16.

54. Robert Nugent, Jeannine Gramick, and Thomas Oddo, *Homosexual Catholics: A New Primer for Discussion* (Washington, D.C.: Dignity, Inc., 1980), 4.

positions on homosexuality," even "before any changes are made in official Church teachings."[55]

Equally misleading are its answers regarding the approach to homosexual acts in Holy Scripture. Sodom was supposedly punished for "the violation of the rules of hospitality." The condemnation to death for homosexual acts in Leviticus (see 18:22, 29) was a result of "the procreative need of the Jewish people" or an attempt to separate Israel from pagan practices involving fertility rites.[56] In his epistles, Saint Paul "is talking about heterosexuals indulging in homosexual practices rather than true homosexual persons." For them, such practices would be as *unnatural* as "for a homosexual to engage in heterosexual behavior."[57]

Asked, "Should Catholic homosexual persons still go to confession?" the authors reply that this obligation applies only to those who "adhere strictly to the present Church teaching" but not those who "are attempting to integrate their sexual orientation into their overall Christian life." They should go to confession only "for having freely violated in a serious matter one's basic commitment or 'fundamental option' to live a life of self-sacrificing love in the manner of Jesus Christ."[58]

Regarding the liturgical celebration of homosexual unions, Fathers Nugent and Oddo and Sister Gramick adopt the radical position of the National Center for Gay Ministry, which, in its booklet *Ministry USA* (1971), suggests, "Eventually gay marriages might be celebrated within the gay community's liturgical celebrations and eventually, even within the traditional parish community."[59]

---

55. Nugent, et al., *Homosexual Catholics*, 7–8.
56. Nugent, 11.
57. Nugent, 12.
58. Nugent, 14.
59. Nugent, 17.

In 1983, Fr. Robert Nugent directed the publication of a collective work titled *A Challenge to Love: Gay and Lesbian Catholics in the Church*. It included an introduction by Most Rev. Walter F. Sullivan, bishop of Richmond, Virginia and contributions from Fr. John McNeill, Sr. Jeannine Gramick, Matthew Fox (a former Dominican expelled from the Order), and thirteen other authors. Fr. Daniel Maguire's contribution was meaningfully titled "The Morality of Homosexual Marriage."

Correctly calling it "a work of advocacy," James Hanigan noted in his review: "Homophobia, Capitalism and Patriarchy are the enemies . . . the homosexual orientation is no longer problematic but a gift from God to heal the world's hurts . . . the norm for judging sexual acts and relations is no longer their unitive-procreative purpose but the personal quality of the relationship . . . practicing homosexuals may be admitted to the Eucharist."[60]

This scholarly offensive resulted in the *New Dictionary of Theology*, published in the U.S.A. in 1987, stating that the Bible does not condemn homosexual activity except when it involves rape, has idolatrous connotations, or violates the requirements of hospitality.

In 1992, Father Nugent and Sister Gramick reiterated their dissent from traditional Catholic doctrine in the book *Building Bridges: Gay & Lesbian Reality and the Catholic Church*, with a foreword by Fr. Charles Curran. Twenty-five years later, their book's title inspired that of Fr. James Martin, who used the metaphor in the singular, which does not require much imagination: *Building a Bridge: How the Catholic Church and the LGBT Community Can Enter Into a Relationship of Respect, Compassion, and Sensitivity.*

---

60. James P. Hanigan, Review of *A Challenge to Love: Gay and Lesbian Catholics in the Church*, ed. Robert Nugent, *Horizons* 11, no. 1 (1984): 203, https://doi.org/10.1017/S0360966900033508203-204.

In Europe, the Homosexual Agenda
Spreads From the Netherlands

In Europe, the Netherlands was a trailblazer in promoting the pro-homosexual agenda in society and the Catholic Church. Since 1946, the officially named Dutch Association for Homophiles, which also included lesbians, was active. It had previously operated under the dissimulating name Cultuur en Ontspanningscentrum – COC ("Center for Culture and Leisure"). In 1958, Catholic priests and psychiatrists opened a help center for homosexuals in Amsterdam, then Europe's most libertine homosexual venue. In 1961, they published a booklet (A. F. C. Overing et al., *Homosexualiteit,* Pastorale Cahiers, 1961, vol. 3) cautiously calling for acceptance. Later, Franciscan J. Gottschalk, one of the help center's animators, contributed as a theologian to the collective ecumenical work *The Church and Homosexuality,* published in 1973.

Earlier, in 1968, the Capuchin Father Herman van de Spijker had published the book titled *Die gleichgeschlechtliche Zuneigung. Homotropie: Homosexualität, Homoerotik, Homophilie, und die katholische Moraltheologie* ("Same-Sex Attraction: Homotropy—Homosexuality, Homoeroticism, Homophilia, and Catholic Moral Theology"), an adaptation of his doctoral thesis at the University of Würzburg, followed four years later by *Homotropie: Menschlichkeit als Rechtfertigung. Überlegungen zur gleichgeschlechtlichen Zuneigung* ("Homotropy: Humanity as a Justification—Considerations on Same-Sex Attraction"), which had a Spanish version titled *Homotropía: Inclinación hacia el mismo sexo,* from which we extract the main ideas.

Within a Freudian conceptual framework ("I," "superego," "personalization," and "sublimation" of the sexual instinct), Fr. van de Spijker uses a passage from the *Summa theologiae* in which Saint Thomas states that the pleasure of sexual commerce between men can be natural for them because of a certain corruption of nature as in the case of a person with a fever who finds bitter food sweet. From this, Fr. van de Spijker deduces that although homosexual acts do not correspond to the order of Creation, they do correspond, however, to "the concrete and factual nature of homotropic man, and are, therefore, in some way natural [for him]."[61] Fr. van de Spijker goes even further than American theologians and pastoral counselors who favor stable monogamous unions to avoid promiscuity, as he finds positive aspects even in "the fleeting evening encounter between two homotropic men in a city park, in which the two satisfy each other sexually. ... There is always—however weakly—a communication, a moment of sympathy" that serves "as a means of calming and giving rest to personal tensions" and "as an outlet of vitality in order to achieve a more relaxed existence." They can even "contribute much to the maturation of a person." In any case, "very often only the person in question can estimate his total situation, concrete nature, and his unique and unrepeatable character."[62]

Contrary to Saint Thomas, for whom homosexual attraction is a corruption of nature, for Fr. van de Spijker, homosexuality is a divine vocation endowed with its own charisms: "This is the place to ask whether homotropy could and should not be given its own meaning and special content. To what extent is this anthropological peculiarity determined by God and directed by nature to a concrete and specific vital task? A theology of vocation and charisms has much to unveil here."[63]

---

61. Herman van de Spijker, *Homotropía: Inclinación hacia el mismo sexo* (Madrid: Sociedad de Educación Atenas, 1976), 36.

62. Van de Spijker, *Homotropía*, 44–45.

63. Van de Spijker, 51.

These questions were probably addressed in discussions held in Catholic parishes and groups from 1979 on by the Catholic Council for Church and Society, a department of the Bishops' Conference of the Netherlands, which published its document titled *Homosexual Persons in Society*.

Cardinal Daneels Kept Silent While the Largest Catholic Magazine in Flanders Helped Welcome Pedophilia

For a long time, *Kerk en Leven* was the weekly magazine with the largest circulation in Flanders (more than half a million copies). It was published under the supervision of the Flemish hierarchy.

In its August 9, 1984 edition, it published an advertisement presenting the activities of the "Ecumenical Working Group on Pedophilia." This group had existed for several years and comprised both Catholics and Protestants. The Working Group's goals included in the ad were as follows:

> This working group wishes to raise awareness among churches about the phenomenon of pedophilia, transmit information, and combat prejudice.
>
> At the same time, the working group intends to learn about everything that is happening in the field of pedophilia.
>
> Finally, the working group wants to create a meeting place for pedophiles to encourage the exchange of ideas and encourage each other.

The group's favorable handling of pedophilia was very clear in the sentence immediately following: "All those who wish to learn more about pedophilia and pedophiles are welcome, provided they do so with openness, respect, and trust."

The ad further mentioned that, with the start of the new season, Fr. Jozef Barzin, a well-known parish priest from Antwerp, would participate in the group's activities.

In October of the same year, a concerned mother sent a letter to Cardinal Godfried Daneels, archbishop of Mechelen-Brussels, complaining about the material offered in the ad and which she had received from the Ecumenical Working

Group on Pedophilia. Her letter went unanswered. Here are some quotes that particularly scandalized her:

- "If your son or daughter feels that the bond with the pedophile is good, do not destroy that bond."
- "The reaction of the environment is often more harmful than the events themselves."
- "Many convinced Christians can learn something from pedophiles."
- "It is preferable that a relationship of trust be established between the pedophile and the parents." [*]

[*] "De allesbehalve katholieke Kerkin Vlaanderen," Rechts Actueel, Jan. 21, 2014, accessed May 8, 2024, https://web.archive.org/web/20171230225903/https://re-act.be/2014/01/21/de-allesbehalve-katholieke-kerk-in-vlaanderen/.

Apparently, Cardinal Daneels just allowed things to continue. Twenty-six years later, in April 2010, he discovered that a friend, Most Rev. Roger Vangheluwe, bishop of Bruges, had sexually abused a nephew for thirteen years, starting when the boy was just five years old. Perhaps inspired by the above-quoted Ecumenical Working Group on Pedophilia's recommendations, at a meeting between the predator, the victim, and the victim's family, Cardinal Daneels tried to convince the abused young man to remain silent.

Although the scandal became public a week or two later, only in March 2024 did Pope Francis finally laicize Roger Vangheluwe.

The same intellectual whirlwind occurred in the rest of Western Europe in the 1970s. For example, in 1975, the French psychoanalyst Fr. Marc Oraison, two of whose works were placed on the Index of Forbidden Books, published his work *The Homosexual Question*. In Ireland, in 1979, the Redemptorist Fr. Ralph Gallagher wrote an article for *The Furrow* magazine titled "Understanding the Homosexual." In 1981, the Spanish Redemptorist Fr. Marciano Vidal directed the publication of a collective work titled *Homosexuality: Science and Conscience.*

The Contribution of Queer Liberation Theology

In their "gay catechism," Fathers Nugent and Oddo and Sister Gramick address the question of what is the right pastoral attitude toward people with a homosexual orientation and answer that it should have the following objectives: "a healthy self-acceptance and self-love and a life of responsible Christian sexual expression in the context of the homosexual orientation and the responsibilities and challenges that flow from that particular human reality." They add: "The paradigm of this position is the 'liberation theology' movement in the Church where groups begin to reflect on their own lived experiences, articulate self-definitions, and engender a sense of pride as individuals and as a group who are responsible for their own lives and contributions to the larger society and Church community."[64]

In fact, in addition to economic, social, racial, and cultural analyses, the new liberation theologies also exploit moral and psychological factors, taking on new homosexual, feminist, and gender-oriented trends. The homosexual cause is indeed an important element of the global Revolution.

Mario Mieli (1952–1983), founder of F.U.O.R.I. (Italian Revolutionary Homosexual United Front) explains, "The gradual liberation of repressed erotic tendencies will further strengthen the revolutionary movement. . . . We cannot imagine the importance of the contribution made to the revolution and human emancipation by the progressive liberation of sadism, masochism, pederasty, gerontophilia, bestiality, autoerotism, fetishism, scatology, undinism, exhibitionism, voyeurism, etc."[65]

---

64. Nugent, *Homosexual Catholics*, 7.
65. Claudia Pilato, "Dall'omosessualità alla pedofilia: sullo scivolo della rivoluzione

The homosexual horizon is not new in Liberation Theology. Canadian Guy Ménard, professor of religious studies at the University of Quebec, was undoubtedly a pioneer. In 1980, he wrote *De Sodome à l'Exode: Jalons pour une théologie de la libération gaie* ("From Sodom to Exodus: Milestones for a Gay Liberation Theology"). Some groups of "Catholic homosexuals," including the European Forum of Homosexual Christians, attended the international conference of liberation theologians held in Madrid in September 1989. A round table was devoted to "groups and sectors marginalized in the Church." The idea was to find new "marginalized groups" to replace the role of *the poor* in the old Liberation Theology, and it included homosexuals, now seen as "moral proletarians." The main lecture was delivered by Fr. Emili Boils, who stated, "I am homosexual by nature and by the grace of God.... I am a priest because I am homosexual." The priest went on to denounce "the twenty centuries of social and religious marginalization, of oppression of every kind which my people have suffered." He closed with a threat: "We must prepare for war, our own intifada."[66]

In subsequent years, by applying Liberation Theology categories to homosexuals and lesbians—deemed "oppressed" and in need of "liberation"—Catholic and Protestant theologians developed gay, lesbian, and queer liberation theology. The expression *queer theology* was coined in 1994 by Robert Goss in his book *Jesus Acted Up: A Gay and Lesbian Manifesto*. Queer theology rests on the assumption that gender nonconformity and homosexual conduct are a constant in history. What is needed is to discover

---

sessuale," *Tradizione Famiglia Proprietà* (Oct. 2013), 18, accessed Apr. 24, 2024, https://issuu.com/tradizionefamigliaproprieta/docs/tfpottobre2013.

66. Julio Loredo, "Homosexualidad y teología de la liberación," *Covadonga Informa* (Madrid, May 1990), 8–9, accessed Apr. 24, 2024, https://issuu.com/nestor87/docs/covadonga_informa_1986_1990. For the written proceedings of the conference, see Joaquín Ruiz-Gimenez, ed., *Iglesia y derechos humanos: IX Congreso de teología* (Madrid: Evangelio y Liberación, 1989).

the "structures of oppression" that have historically weighed upon these categories and proclaim their "liberation."[67]

Latin America Is Not Left Out of the Pro-Homosexual Offensive

In 1967, *Vozes* magazine, published by the Franciscans of Petrópolis, state of Rio de Janeiro, carried an article by Dutch Redemptorist Jaime Snoek, who lived in Brazil, titled *Eles também são da nossa estirpe: Considerações sobre a homofilia* ("They're Our Kind Too: Considerations on Homophilia"). In this article about homosexual practice, he affirmed that insofar as it promoted an oblative love in the people involved, it could not a priori be qualified as immoral and against nature.

In 1985, the Jesuit *Edições Loyola* published a translation of the book directed by Fr. Marciano Vidal, while *Vozes* published *Sexualidade, libertação e fé: Por uma erótica cristã* ("Sexuality, Liberation and Faith: For a Christian Erotica"), by feminist liberation theologian Rose Marie Muraro, a disciple of Bishop Helder Câmara and ex-Franciscan friar Leonardo Boff. In 2005, the Brazilian Congress awarded Muraro the title "Matron of Brazilian Feminism." In 1988, *Perspectiva Teológica,* another journal linked to the Jesuits, published "Homosexuals and Liberation Ethics" by Fr. Bernardino Leers, a Dutch Franciscan living in Brazil. Two years later, the publishing house linked to the Shrine of Our Lady of Aparecida published the article "Understanding the Homosexual" by the abovementioned Irish Redemptorist Fr. Raphael Gallagher in booklet format.

---

67. See John J. McNeill, *Scommettere su Dio, teologia della liberazione omosessuale* (Casale Monferrato: Edizioni Sonda, 1994); Patrick S. Cheng, *Radical Love: An Introduction to Queer Theology* (New York: Church Publishing, 2011); Robert E. Goss, *Take Back the Word: A Queer Reading of the Bible* (Boston: The Pilgrim Press, 2000); Gary David Comstock, *Gay Theology Without Apology* (Cleveland, Oh.: The Pilgrim Press, 1993); J. Michael Clark, *A Place to Start: Toward an Unapologetic Gay Liberation Theology* (Monument, Colo.: Monument Publishing, 1989).

CHAPTER 5

Catholic Homosexuals Come Out of the Closet and Influence the Debate

This theological *fifth column* within Catholic ranks served as a justification to create groups led chiefly by priests and nuns to promote the homosexual cause within the Church under the pretext of pastoral care for same-sex pairs.

On February 11, 1971, Fr. Patrick Nidorf, an Augustinian priest and psychologist from San Diego, started monthly self-help meetings for homosexuals and lesbians in the basement of St. Brendan's Church in Los Angeles and called the group *Dignity*. Its first constitution, "written in May 1970, argued that 'homosexuality is a natural variation on the use of sex' and that gays and lesbians could be proud of their 'responsible and fulfilling' experiences of sexual intimacy."[68] The local archbishop censured the initiative because the group affirmed the goodness of same-sex relationships and celebrated gay and lesbian identities. Father Nidorf then handed leadership over to the laity. It was the first group of its kind in the Catholic Church in the United States.

In 1974, Fr. Robert Nugent and Sr. Jeannine Gramick took over as Dignity chaplains. Three years later, without leaving that post, the two co-founded a similar group called New Ways Ministry. The name was inspired by a phrase from Bishop Francis J. Mugavero's pastoral letter to his faithful in the diocese of Brooklyn, New York, titled *Sexuality—God's Gift*. In the pastoral letter, Bishop Mugavero assured them of the hierarchy's willingness to try to find "new ways" of evangelizing that would free homosexuals from discrimination.

---

68. Jason Steidl Jack, "Remembering Revolutionary Pax Nidorf, Who Founded LGBT Ministry DignityUSA," *National Catholic Reporter*, Apr. 11, 2023, https://www.ncronline.org /opinion/guest-voices/remembering-revolutionary-pax-nidorf-who-founded-lgbt-ministry -dignityusa.

Similar groups, some proclaiming themselves Catholic and others ecumenical, sprouted like mushrooms in many countries. Some worth mentioning are *David & Jonathan* (France, 1972), *Acceptance* (Australia, 1972), *Quest* (United Kingdom, 1973), *Communauté du Christ libérateur* (Belgium, 1974) and *Homosexuelle und Kirche* (Germany, 1977).

In 2003, the Coordination of Christian Homosexual Groups in Italy (C.O.C.I.) was established to network the various groups of Christian homosexuals active in that country. Several Catholic homosexual groups, such as Ali d'Aquila and L.G.B.T. Christians, came out of the closet and took part in "Gay Pride" parades. "If one does not overcome the barriers of the mind, those of the heart will have a hard time. That is why for many centuries our church found it hard to accept homosexual love," declared theologian Vito Mancuso at the Forum of Homosexual Christians held in May 2012 at the Somascan Fathers' house in Albano (Rome), at the request of volunteers of the Gionata Project.[69]

In Brazil, the first organized group of people identifying as "L.G.B.T. Catholics" emerged in 2007 in Rio de Janeiro and adopted the name *Catholic Diversity*. It inspired the founding of many similar groups throughout the country. In 2014, the National Network of L.G.B.T. Catholic Groups was created. It is currently made up of more than twenty groups and is part of the Global Network of Rainbow Catholics (G.N.R.C.) from around the world, created in Rome during the opening week of the Synod on the Family in October 2015.

These pro-homosexual groups calling themselves Catholic or Christian serve as the homosexual movement's fellow

---

69. Pasquale Quaranta, "Chiesa e omosessualità, intervista a Vito Mancuso," Liberstef .myblog.it, May 8, 2012. For the complete text of Mancuso's speech, see Progetto Gionata, "Il teologo Mancuso e le prospettive teologiche sull'amore omosessuale e il suo esercizio mediante l'affettività," Progetto Gionata, Apr. 27, 2012.

travelers. They participate in their campaigns and events, especially "Gay Pride" parades and take up all their demands, especially the legal recognition of unnatural unions. But their main tactical objective is to help tear down the barriers of horror and repudiation that the *sensus fidei* of Catholics raises as a psychological defense against unnatural, depraved relationships. By breaking down those barriers, these groups favor the "moral revolution aimed at changing people's view of homosexuality," as mentioned by John Varnell.

One of the main strategies of homosexual propaganda is to encourage "coming out of the closet" by those who live in unnatural partnerships or lead an unbridled sexual life. In the 1989 book *After the Ball*, Marshall Kirk and Hunter Madsen call for "a program of unabashed propaganda, firmly grounded in long-established principles of psychology and advertising."[70]

One of the program's main aspects is to "desensitize, jam, and/or convert"[71] the centrist sector of the population while, at the same time, "encourage the largest possible number of homosexuals and lesbians from all walks of life and professions, especially celebrities, to 'come out.' This creates insecurity in the public's rejection of homosexuality."[72]

A study published in Brazil corroborates this strategy. Researcher Cristiana de Assis Serra, in her dissertation titled "'Viemos pra comungar': Estratégias de permanência na Igreja desenvolvidas por grupos de 'católicos LGBT' brasileiros e suas implicações" (We Came to Receive Communion: Strategies for Remaining in the Church Developed by Brazilian 'LGBT

---

70. Kirk and Madsen, *After the Ball*, xxvi.

71. Kirk and Madsen, 173.

72. TFP Committee on American Issues, *Defending a Higher Law: Why We Must Resist Same-sex "Marriage" and the Homosexual Movement* (Spring Grove, Penn.: The American Society for the Defense of Tradition, Family, and Property—TFP, 2004), 34, accessed Apr. 24, 2024, https://www.tfp.org/images/books/Defending_A_Higher_Law.pdf.

Catholic' Groups and Their Implications) devotes an entire
section to the theme: "The (double) coming out of the closet
as appropriation of space and subversion of order." In it, the
author explains that, when choosing the name of the group
and its website, the founders of Catholic Diversity in the city
of Rio de Janeiro opted for a "gradual visibility increase": "If
its name alone already constituted a 'coming out of the closet'
even if slowly 'opening the door,' the slogan at the top of the
website's homepage made it clear: 'For gays to live their vocation and dignity as children of God in the Church and society.'"

According to the researcher, the result is that "by self-
identifying as 'diverse,' those hitherto considered 'excluded'
are made visible in their materiality within and not outside
the religious field," thus disproving "the supposed uniformity
of the Roman Catholic camp."

In contrast to the previous "fearful concealment and fear of
involuntary exposure," Catholic Diversity "makes itself visible
and deliberately names itself as a 'movement of practicing
gay Catholics,'" subverting the hierarchical, verticalized "clerical order that had prevailed until then and legitimized those
holding power to define 'good' and 'bad,' the 'norm' and its
'deviation,' 'inclusion' and 'exclusion.'"[73]

A paradigmatic example of this subversive strategy was
the coming out of the first Dutch public figure, the novelist
and poet Gerard Kornelis van het Reve (alias Gerard), who, in
a 1963 interview on national television, spoke about his sexual
orientation. At the same time, he converted from atheism to
Catholicism and was baptized in 1966, even though the pre-

---

73. Cristiana de Assis Serra, " 'Viemos pra comungar': Estratégias de permanência
na Igreja desenvolvidas por grupos de 'católicos LGBT' brasileiros e suas implicações"
(master's thesis, Universidade do Estado do Rio de Janeiro, 2017), 107–111, accessed
Apr. 21, 2024, https://www.diversidadesexual.com.br/wp-content/uploads/2013/04/Cat
%C3%B3licos-LGBT-Cristiana-Serra.pdf.

vious year, he had been charged with blasphemy for having written that God's next incarnation would be as a donkey, with which he, Gerard, would have anal intercourse. In 1968, the Supreme Court acquitted him, and the following year, he was granted the State Prize for Dutch Literature.

Three months later, the prestigious Society of Dutch Literature staged a public tribute, broadcast live on national television, which took place in an Amsterdam Catholic church. The show ended with the author walking down the church aisle hand in hand with his then-boyfriend. "Two weeks after 'the greatest show in church,' van het Reve participated in a panel discussion on 'emotions about homophilia,' hosted by the Catholic College for Theology and Pastorate. [On] this occasion, he voiced his pessimism about the social acceptance of homosexuality but proved quite optimistic about development[s] in Dutch Catholicism: 'It looks like the church will recognize monogamous homophile relationships.' The college's professor of ethics agreed with this and urged pastors to comply if a homophile couple requested 'sanctification' of their relationship—a call that did not go unnoticed by the press."[74]

74. David J. Bos, "'Equal Rites Before the Law': Religious Celebrations of Same-Sex Relationships in the Netherlands, 1960s–1990s," *Theology & Sexuality* 23, no. 3 (2017): 197, https://www.tandfonline.com/doi/full/10.1080/13558358.2017.1351123.

CHAPTER 6

The Church Caught Between the Brutal Pincer Jaws of Defiance and Blackmail

The homosexual movement's combined pressure inside and outside the Church is exerted mainly through defiance and blackmail.

Defiance seeks to denounce the Catholic Church's doctrine and authorities through attention-grabbing cases spread by the mainstream media in which homosexual activists appear as victims. This creates the idea among the public that Church doctrine and authorities are discriminatory and offensive toward good people whose only handicap is same-sex attraction.

The Netherlands was the first country in which members of the Catholic hierarchy suffered a systematic onslaught with this confrontational technique. In 1979, Bishop Joannes Gijsen of Roermond declared that those living the homosexual lifestyle should not come to church and present themselves for the sacraments. "Thousands of [homosexual] and lesbian activists marched against the bishop on the Saturday before Easter, which they dubbed 'Pink Saturday.'"[75]

The first international example of this strategy was the Rainbow Sash Movement,[76] which began in England, where Nick Holloway was the first homosexual Catholic to wear a rainbow sash during Mass. From the U.K., it spread to Australia, where, in 1997, Most Rev. George Pell, archbishop of Melbourne, refused to give Holy Communion during Mass to two openly homosexual Catholic men, one of whom was a priest.

---

75. Bos, *Equal Rites*, 193.

76. See Wikipedia contributors, "Rainbow Sash Movement," Wikipedia, The Free Encyclopedia, accessed Apr. 21, 2024, https://en.wikipedia.org/w/index.php?title=Rainbow _Sash_Movement&oldid=1160411803.

In response, at the Pentecost Sunday Mass the following year, a group of seventy people wearing rainbow sashes presented themselves ostentatiously for Communion, which Archbishop Pell denied, something he courageously did in that city on ten other occasions. After his transfer to the Sidney archdiocese, on the first Pentecost, a group of about twenty homosexuals came forward to receive Communion, creating an incident widely reported in the media. Immediately after Mass, Michael Kelly, a Rainbow Sash spokesman and former Franciscan seminarian, revealed to the crowd the tactical aim of that challenge: "We're here to break the code of silence and invisibility that the church has imposed on gay and lesbian people as their price for involvement in the church for so many centuries."[77]

The movement spread from Australia to the United States. The movement's leaders justified the choice of Pentecost for their actions and confrontation by claiming that the Holy Spirit distributed a great diversity of gifts on that occasion, including homosexuality. If denied Communion, they returned to their pews and stood in protest.

In 2005, faced with the proliferation of clashes organized by the Rainbow Sash Movement, the secretary of Cardinal Francis Arinze, then-prefect of the Congregation for Divine Worship, wrote in the cardinal's name that "Rainbow Sash wearers . . . are showing their opposition to Church teaching on a major issue of natural law, and so disqualify themselves from being given Holy Communion."[78] The following year, the cardinal himself reaffirmed his denial in an interview with E.W.T.N.:

---

77. "Pell Lashes Out After Gays Refused Communion," *The Sydney Morning Herald*, May 20, 2002, https://www.smh.com.au/national/pell-lashes-out-after-gays-refused-communion-20020520-gdfakf.html.

78. Matt Abbott, "The 'Rainbow Sash Movement' Controversy," Catholic Online, accessed Apr. 21, 2024, https://www.catholic.org/featured/headline.php?ID=2121&page=2.

These rainbow sash people are really saying, 'We are homosexuals, we intend to remain so and we want to receive
Holy Communion.'

The *Catechism of the Catholic Church* . . . says it is not condemning a person for having homosexual tendency. We don't
condemn anybody for that. But a person stands condemned
for acting on it.[79]

Unfortunately, on the ground, many priests and eucharistic ministers lacked the same courage as Cardinals Pell and
Arinze. Worse still, some bishops invited them to come with
their banners to cathedral Masses. For example, shortly before
Pentecost 2005, the animator of the Rainbow Sash Movement
in the U.S.A. was contacted by the Director of Media Relations
for the archdiocese of Los Angeles to inform him, on behalf
of Cardinal Roger Mahony, that "members of the Rainbow
Sash Movement who come to the Cathedral of Our Lady of
the Angels this Sunday will be most welcome to attend any
of our Masses."[80]

Another example of this defiance technique, one with
huge media repercussions, was the incident caused by
Barbara Johnson, an American lesbian living in Maryland. Her
mother, a parishioner at St. John Neumann Church, died in
2012, one week after the approval of homosexual "marriage"
in that state. Johnson entered the sacristy with her lesbian
partner immediately before the funeral Mass and told the
young celebrant that the two had been living together for
nineteen years. Her spontaneous declaration of living in public
sin forced the young parochial vicar to discreetly refuse her
Communion during Mass. She made a scandal and received

---

79. "Rainbow Sash Members to Disrupt Masses Across US, Again," *Catholic Exchange*,
May 26, 2007, https://catholicexchange.com/rainbow-sash-members-to-disrupt-masses
-across-us-again/.

80. Terence Weldon, "Rainbow Sash Movement," QueeringtheChurch.wordpress.com, Mar.
6, 2010, https://queeringthechurch.wordpress.com/2010/03/06/rainbow-sash-movement/.

from a lay minister who was distributing the Holy Eucharist to another line. Faced with that insult, the young priest refused to accompany the funeral procession to the cemetery.[81]

The incident created a national media scandal in which the priest was spun as the villain. Conversely, the lay Eucharistic minister and other Catholic attendees immediately sympathized with the lesbian daughter and were presented as heroes. So was the parish priest. He called Johnson to apologize upon learning of the incident. However, the media's main "hero" was the archdiocese of Washington, where the parish is located. It issued a statement repudiating the young priest's attitude, although he did nothing but apply what the Code of Canon Law says should be done when public sinners seek to receive Holy Communion (can. 915). Worse still, the archdiocese suspended the priest from ministry two weeks later, supposedly for unrelated reasons![82]

Thus, the way was practically open for pro-homosexual activists to come forward to receive Communion in similar situations, putting priests and Eucharistic ministers in such an embarrassing situation that many ended up giving in for fear of the media . . . and the bishop.

In addition to media scandals, the defiance technique took a step forward when, taking advantage of new legislation equating so-called hate crimes with racism and including "sexual minorities" among classes of people especially protected

81. See Michelle Boorstein, "D.C. Archdiocese: Denying Communion to Lesbian at Funeral Was Against 'Policy,'" *Washington Post*, Feb. 29, 2012, https://www.washingtonpost.com /local/dc-archdiocese-denying-communion-to-lesbian-at-funeral-was-against-policy/2012 /02/28/gIQAIlxVgR_story.html.

82. See Jerry Filteau, "Priest Who Denied Lesbian Woman Communion Suspended for Other Reasons," *National Catholic Reporter*, Mar. 13, 2012, https://www.ncronline.org/news /people/priest-who-denied-lesbian-woman-communion-suspended-other-reasons; Luiz Sérgio Solimeo, "The Homosexual Movement Scores a Win in the Fr. Guarnizo Affair—Who Caused the Scandal and Why?" TFP.org, Mar. 17, 2012, https://www.tfp.org/the-homosexual -movement-scores-a-win-in-the-fr-guarnizo-affair-who-caused-the-scandal-and-why/.

against discrimination, the homosexual movement moved on to accusations of "homophobia" in the courts.

In the Catholic camp, the case of Most Rev. Juan Antonio Reig Plá, bishop of Alcalá de Henares in Spain, was a paradigmatic example of this judicial offensive. He declared in a 2012 Good Friday sermon broadcast on a Spanish public television channel that young men who are disoriented by gender ideology, think they are attracted to people of the same sex, and go to men's nightclubs to experience it, "find hell."[83]

Immediately, the State Federation of Lesbians, Gays, Transsexuals, and Bisexuals (F.E.L.G.T.B.) filed an incitement of contempt complaint against the bishop with Madrid's district attorney. The trial judge dismissed the complaint after Bishop Reig Plá received hundreds of letters of support for his statements from people who confessed to having experienced the "hell" described in his sermon.[84] A micro-political party lodged an appeal, which a Madrid Court rejected.[85] However, the whole judicial affair disrupted the bishop's life and ministry for two years and aroused a section of Spanish society against him, which intimidated other prelates into silence.

A different manifestation of defiance with a global reach was the organization of the first World Pride march in Rome by Interpride. This association brings together organizers of national "Gay Pride" marches. It held its Rome march during

83. "El obispo de Alcalá de Henares carga contra los homosexuales y el aborto en la misa de TVE," CadenaSer.com, Apr. 7, 2012, https://cadenaser.com/ser/2012/04/07/espana/1333756218_850215.html.

84. See "La Fiscalía archiva la denuncia de la FELGTB contra el obispo de Alcalá," La Información, May 9, 2012, https://www.lainformacion.com/asuntos-sociales/la-fiscalia-archiva-la-denuncia-de-la-felgtb-contra-el-obispo-de-alcala_s6bwExtK8dogjgEwaDQGa2/.

85. See "El obispo de Alcalá ejerció su libertad de expresión al criticar a gays durante una homilía en 2012," El Mundo, May 16, 2014, https://www.elmundo.es/madrid/2014/05/16/5375b18fca47417b188b456c.html.

the Jubilee of the Holy Year 2000. The parade brought together thousands of people who shouted slogans through the streets of the Eternal City. On the same day, Pope John Paul II felt compelled to address the crowd in St. Peter's Square: "In the name of the church of Rome, I cannot not express bitterness for the affront to the Grand Jubilee of the year 2000 and for the offense to the Christian values of a city that is so dear to the hearts of Catholics across the world."[86]

Confrontation is not the only way to break Catholic resistance, though. Another is blackmail. Historically, this has taken two forms. On the one hand, denouncing the supposed hypocrisy of the Catholic Church because it preaches against homosexuality while many prelates frequent bars and saunas that function as same-sex brothels. The most notorious case is Frédéric Martel's book *Sodoma*, which alleges "The Vatican has one of the world's most numerous gay communities, and I doubt there are as many homos even in San Francisco's Castro district—that iconic gay neighborhood—which is now more mixed!"[87]

Such accusations sometimes lead to the resignation of those forced to "come out of the closet" against their will, as happened in 2002 with Most Rev. Rembert Weakland, archbishop of Milwaukee, Wisconsin, after it was revealed that he used $450,000 in archdiocesan funds to settle a complaint of sexual assault.[88]

---

86. Alessandra Stanley, "Pope Declares His 'Bitterness' Over Gay Event, *The New York Times*, Jul. 10, 2000, https://www.nytimes.com/2000/07/10/world/pope-declares-his-bitterness-over-gay-event.html.

87. Thomas Mahler, "Exclusif: 'Sodoma', le livre-choc sur l'homosexualité au Vatican, *Lepoint.fr*, Feb. 13, 2019, https://www.lepoint.fr/societe/exclusif-sodoma-le-livre-choc-sur-l-homosexualite-au-vatican-13-02-2019-2293213_23.php.

88. See Associated Press, "Ex-Archbishop Apologizes for Payment Scandal," *Washington Post*, May 31, 2002, https://www.washingtonpost.com/archive/politics/2002/06/01/ex-archbishop-apologizes-for-payment-scandal/3f91ad2b-baee-4c0c-a659-4c4560a50a54/.

The same happened to Cardinal Hans Hermann Groer, archbishop of Vienna. In March 1995, he was accused of sexually abusing seminarians. Six months later, Pope John Paul II accepted his resignation.[89] In February 2013, Cardinal Keith O'Brien, leader of the Catholic Church in Scotland, was forced to resign three months before the age limit due to allegations of inappropriate acts with four priests during the 1980s and later.[90]

In another form of blackmail, certain pro-homosexual groups and leaders began pressuring prelates to dissent publicly from Vatican documents and sanctions. Perhaps the most paradigmatic case is that of Cardinal Basil Hume. In April 1995, Peter Tatchell, leader of OutRage!, an association that forced several high-ranking Anglicans "out of the closet," pressured him publicly. Fr. Richard John Neuhaus, founder of the well-known magazine *First Things*, recounts what happened to the English cardinal almost thirty years ago: "Mr. Tatchell had been demanding that Hume back down from Rome's definition of homosexual acts as 'objectively disordered.' The demands sometimes became violent, disrupting the Palm Sunday procession at Westminster Cathedral. In what was perceived to be a response to the pressure, the Cardinal issued a letter that said homosexual friendship can be 'a way of loving' and declared that 'homophobia should have no place among Catholics.' The papers predictably headlined the Cardinal's 'capitulation' to gay pressure groups. Even the conservative *Telegraph* put on the front page, 'Cardinal Hume gives Church blessing to homosexual love.'"[91]

---

89. See Dennis Coday, "A Cardinal Is Accused: The Groer Case," *National Catholic Reporter*, Apr. 4, 2014, https://www.ncronline.org/blogs/ncr-today/cardinal-accused-groer-case.

90. See Isla Binnie, "Pope Accepts Disgraced Cardinal O'Brien's Resignation From Public Role," *Reuters*, Mar. 20, 2015, https://www.reuters.com/article/idUSKBN0MG20U/.

91. Richard John Neuhaus, "Primrose Paths," in "A Sense of Change Both Ominous and

OutRage! could claim that its campaign was successful in determining not only the Church of England's policy on homosexuality but also that of the Catholic Church. Alas, Mr. Tatchell was correct in boasting to the *New York Times*: "We are setting the agenda."[92]

In fact, in a press release, the then-archbishop of Westminster, expanding on an earlier statement from 1993, declared, "In whatever context it arises, and always respecting the appropriate manner of its expression, love between two persons, whether of the same sex or a different sex, is to be treasured and respected," since "to love another . . . is to have entered the area of the richest human experience, whether that love is between persons of the same sex or of a different sex." He concluded, "Although homosexual genital acts are objectively wrong, nonetheless, the Church warns against generalizations in attributing culpability in individual cases."[93]

Promising," *First Things*, Aug. 1995, https://www.firstthings.com/article/1995/08/a-sense-of-change-both-ominous-and-promising.

92. John Darnton, "Gay Issue Roils the Church of England," *The New York Times*, Mar. 19, 1995, https://www.nytimes.com/1995/03/19/world/gay-issue-roils-church-of-england.html.

93. Basil Hume, "A Note on the Teaching of the Catholic Church Concerning Homosexuality" (Apr. 1997), nos. 9, 10, and 16, New Ways Ministry, accessed Apr. 22, 2024, https://www.newwaysministry.org/wp-content/uploads/2018/12/Hume1997.pdf.

CHAPTER 7

The Holy See Reiterates That Homosexual Acts Are "Grave Depravities"

Holy See dicasteries held the doctrinal line unchanged even though many bishops in various countries caved to homosexual lobby pressure by making weak or ambiguous statements on the pastoral care for homosexual individuals.

In 1975, Vatican authorities learned through the leadership of the Society of Jesus that Fr. John McNeill had requested an imprimatur for his book. This prompted the Congregation for the Doctrine of the Faith to publish the declaration *Persona humana* "on certain questions concerning sexual ethics," signed by its prefect, Cardinal Franjo Seper. After recalling that "the use of the sexual function has its true meaning and moral rectitude only in true marriage," the declaration rejects the claim that the tendency in those with an ingrained homosexual attraction is so natural as to justify sexual relations practiced within a community of life. It reiterates, "According to the objective moral order, homosexual relations are acts which lack an essential and indispensable finality. In Sacred Scripture, they are condemned as a serious depravity" and "can in no case be approved of."[94]

This was followed, in 1986, by the *Letter to Bishops of the Catholic Church on the Pastoral Care of Homosexual Persons*, signed by the new prefect of the Congregation for the Doctrine of the Faith, Cardinal Joseph Ratzinger. The document, already quoted in the Introduction, recognizes that "increasing numbers of people today, even within the Church, are bringing enormous pressure to bear on the Church to accept the

---

94. Congregation for the Doctrine of the Faith, declaration *Persona humana* (Dec. 29, 1975), nos. V and VIII, https://www.vatican.va/roman_curia/congregations/cfaith/documents/rc_con_cfaith_doc_19751229_persona-humana_en.html.

homosexual condition as though it were not disordered and to condone homosexual activity."[95] It particularly denounces the fact that "the movement within the Church, which takes the form of pressure groups of various names and sizes, attempts to give the impression that it represents all homosexual persons who are Catholics," but gathers "homosexual persons who have no intention of abandoning their homosexual behavior" (no. 9).

In the face of this movement's concerted offensive, the document reiterates that, although someone's same-sex attraction is not in itself a sin, it is a tendency to behavior that is intrinsically evil from a moral point of view, and therefore, "the inclination itself must be seen as an objective disorder" (no. 3). Concerning homosexual behavior, Cardinal Ratzinger notes that the Church's doctrine is based "not on isolated phrases" of the Bible, "but on the solid foundation of a constant Biblical testimony" that cannot be interpreted "in a way which contradicts the Church's living Tradition" (no. 5). Therefore, "her clear position cannot be revised by pressure from civil legislation or the trend of the moment" (no. 9) and reminds same-sex attracted individuals that they "are called, as all of us are, to a chaste life" (no. 12).

Because of the above, the Congregation for the Doctrine of the Faith asks all bishops "to be especially cautious of any programs which may seek to pressure the Church to change her teaching, even while claiming not to do so" (no. 14). It commands, "All support should be withdrawn from any organizations which seek to undermine the teaching of the Church, which are ambiguous about it, or which neglect it entirely" (no. 17).

---

95. Congregation for the Doctrine of the Faith, *Letter to the Bishops*, no. 8.

In 1992, Pope John Paul II published the *Catechism of the Catholic Church*, which contains a section on "Chastity and Homosexuality" (nos. 2357–2359). The text affirms that "basing itself on Sacred Scripture, which presents homosexual acts as acts of grave depravity, tradition has always declared that 'homosexual acts are intrinsically disordered.' They are contrary to the natural law" (no. 2357).[96] And, further, that the same-sex attraction from which they derive "is 'objectively disordered'" (no. 2358).

To these incontrovertible pronouncements, the Congregation for the Doctrine of the Faith added condemnations of the principal authors who denied the traditional teaching:

–   In 1979, its then-prefect, Cardinal Seper, congratulated the U.S. Conference of Catholic Bishops for denouncing the errors contained in the book *Human Sexuality: New Directions in American Catholic Thought*, edited by Fr. Anthony Kosnik, particularly concerning "the unacceptability of its 'pastoral guidelines' as suitable norms for the formation of Christian consciences in matters of sexual morality."[97]

–   In 1986, after a three-year investigation, Fr. Charles Curran was banned from teaching theology in ecclesiastical institutions in light of his "repeated refusal to accept what the Church teaches," namely "on a right to public dissent from the ordinary Magisterium, the indissolubility of consummated sacramental marriage, abortion, euthanasia, masturbation, arti-

---

96. *Catechism of the Catholic Church*, no. 2357, https://www.vatican.va/archive/ENG 0015/__P85.HTM.

97. Congregation for the Doctrine of the Faith, "Letter to Archbishop John R. Quinn, President of the National Conference of Catholic Bishops in the U.S.A." (Jul. 13, 1979), Vatican.va, https://www.vatican.va/roman_curia/congregations/cfaith/documents/rc_con _cfaith_doc_19790713_mons-quinn_en.html.

ficial contraception, premarital intercourse and homosexual acts."[98]

- Four years later, the same Congregation demanded that Fr. André Guindon retract his book *The Sexual Creators,* in which he inaugurates a concept of "sexual fecundity" (no. 2.1) "independent of 'biological fecundity'" (no. 2.1) and consisting of "'sensuality' and 'tenderness'" (no. 2.1). This concept becomes "the criterion for judging any kind of sexual activity, not only conjugal, nor heterosexual only, but also homosexual" (no. 2.1). Furthermore, "Father Guindon defends the 'sexual fecundity' of homosexuals, claiming to prescind thereby from any judgment on the objective morality of erotic or genital acts they may perform" (no. 2.5). "In some respects, a homosexual relationship would indeed seem to be superior to a heterosexual relationship" (no. 2.5) since homosexuals are "a source of witness to our society in their celebration of gratuitous love" (no. 2.5). On top of that, "the author holds that the moral norms contained in Sacred Scripture should be referred to their historical context in such a way that they are to be considered 'inconclusive' with regard to making a moral judgment today, for example, on homosexual acts" (no. 2.4).[99]

- In 1999, the Congregation issued a "Notification Regarding Sister Jeannine Gramick, S.S.N.D., and Father Robert Nugent, S.D.S.," reporting that neither had respected the ban, communicated fifteen years earlier,

---

98. Congregation for the Doctrine of the Faith, "Letter to Father Charles Curran" (Jul. 25, 1986), Vatican.va, https://www.vatican.va/roman_curia/congregations/cfaith/documents/rc_con_cfaith_doc_19860725_carlo-curran_en.html.

99. Congregation for the Doctrine of the Faith, "Note on the Book by Fr. André Guindon, O.M.I. 'The Sexual Creators, an Ethical Proposal for Concerned Christians" (Jan. 31, 1992), Vatican.va, https://www.vatican.va/roman_curia/congregations/cfaith/documents/rc_con_cfaith_doc_19920131_book-guindon_en.html.

"to separate themselves totally and completely from *New Ways Ministry*, adding that they were not to exercise any apostolate without faithfully presenting the Church's teaching regarding the intrinsic evil of homosexual acts." "Despite this action by the Holy See, Father Nugent and Sister Gramick continued their involvement in activities organized by *New Ways Ministry*, though removing themselves from leadership positions. They also continued to maintain and promote ambiguous positions on homosexuality and explicitly criticized documents of the Church's Magisterium on this issue." Invited to "respond unequivocally to certain questions regarding their position on the morality of homosexual acts and on the homosexual inclination" "Sister Gramick and Father Nugent demonstrated a clear conceptual understanding of the Church's teaching on homosexuality, but refrained from professing any adherence to that teaching." In addition, both "had sought to justify the publication of their books and neither had expressed personal adherence to the Church's teaching on homosexuality in sufficiently unequivocal terms." "Asked to express their interior assent to the teaching of the Catholic Church on homosexuality and to acknowledge that [their] books contained errors," Sister Gramick "simply refused to express any assent whatsoever to the teaching of the Church on homosexuality," and Father Nugent was "not unequivocal in his statement" and later refused to sign a declaration of assent prepared for him. The declaration concludes: "Given the failure of the repeated attempts of the Church's legitimate authorities to resolve the problems presented by the writings and pastoral activities of the two authors, the Congregation for the Doctrine of the Faith is obliged to declare for the good of the Catholic faithful that the positions advanced by Sister Jeannine

Gramick and Father Robert Nugent regarding the intrinsic evil of homosexual acts and the objective disorder of the homosexual inclination are doctrinally unacceptable."[100]

- In 2001, with the signature of Cardinal Ratzinger, the Congregation published a "Notification Regarding Certain Writings of Fr. Marciano Vidal, C.Ss.R.," namely his books *Diccionario de ética teológica: La propuesta moral de Juan Pablo II* and the volumes of *Moral de actitudes*. The notification affirms that these works cannot be used for theological formation, reports on the stages of the investigation, and the author's commitment to correct the errors contained in his works including that in the moral evaluation of homosexuality, one must "'adopt a provisional attitude' formulated 'from the perspective of inquiry and openness'"; and that "for the person who is irreversibly homosexual, a coherent Christian commitment 'does not necessarily lead to the rigid morality of either becoming heterosexual or total abstinence.'"[101]

Another document that particularly infuriated the Church's enemies was the 2002 letter from the Congregation for Divine Worship, signed by Cardinal Jorge Medina Estévez, stating that "The ordination to the diaconate and the priesthood of homosexual men or those with a homosexual tendency is absolutely inadvisable and imprudent and very risky from a pastoral point of view. Therefore, a homosexual or a person with a homosexual tendency is not suitable to receive the

---

100. Congregation for the Doctrine of the Faith, "Notification Regarding Sister Jeannine Gramick, SSND, and Father Robert Nugent, SDS (May 31, 1999), Vatican.va, https://www.vatican.va/roman_curia/congregations/cfaith/documents/rc_con_cfaith_doc_19990531_gramick-nugent-notification_en.html.

101. Congregation for the Doctrine of the Faith, "Notification Regarding Certain Writings of Fr. Marciano Vidal, C.Ss.R." (Feb. 22, 2001), no. 2, Vatican.va, https://www.vatican.va/roman_curia/congregations/cfaith/documents/rc_con_cfaith_doc_20010515_vidal_po.html.

sacrament of Holy Orders."[102] This ban was later confirmed by the Congregation for Catholic Education, responsible for seminaries, in an Instruction signed by Cardinal Zenon Grocholewski and published in November 2005.[103]

At the same time, the Holy See founded or enhanced institutions aimed explicitly at defending and spreading chastity, indissoluble marriage, and the family, such as The Pontifical Council for the Family. Between 1983 and 2008, it was presided over by two conservative cardinals, Their Eminences Édouard Gagnon and Alfonso López Trujillo. In 1995, it published "The Truth and Meaning of Human Sexuality—Guidelines for Education Within the Family."[104] In 1981, the Holy See founded the John Paul II Pontifical Theological Institute for Marriage and Family Sciences.

Other Vatican bodies, however, unable to sanction dissidents with the same energy, adopted an attitude of complacency toward these and other authors. They favored the spread of doctrinal ambiguity and unease with the papacy in Catholic circles, which may have played some role in Benedict XVI's unexpected resignation.

---

102. Congregation for Divine Worship and the Discipline of the Sacraments, "Negativa a la ordenación de homosexuales al sacerdocio" (May 16, 2002), Corazones.org, accessed Apr. 22, 2024, https://www.corazones.org/sacramentos/orden_sac/homosexualidad_ordenacion _2005.htm.

103. See Congregation for Catholic Education, "Instruction Concerning the Criteria for the Discernment of Vocations With Regard to Persons With Homosexual Tendencies in View of Their Admission to the Seminary and to Holy Orders" (Nov. 4, 2005), Vatican.va, https:// www.vatican.va/roman_curia/congregations/ccatheduc/documents/rc_con_ccatheduc_doc _20051104_istruzione_en.html.

104. Pontifical Council for the Family, "The Truth and Meaning of Human Sexuality— Guidelines for Education Within the Family" (Dec. 8, 1995), Vatican.va, https://www.vatican .va/roman_curia/pontifical_councils/family/documents/rc_pc_family_doc_08121995_human -sexuality_po.html.

CHAPTER 8

The Walls of the Dam Start Breaking . . .

Things changed with Cardinal Jorge Mario Bergoglio's ascension to the pontifical throne in March 2013. In July of that year, Pope Francis's famous response on the return flight from World Youth Day in Rio de Janeiro prompted a veritable stampede.

Ilze Scamparini, TV Globo's Rome correspondent, referred to news about Msgr. Battista Ricca's homosexual scandals in Montevideo (he was later appointed administrator of the new papal residence, Casa Santa Marta). She asked Pope Francis how he would approach "the whole question of the gay lobby." The answer to that last question, printed in big headlines in the world's leading newspapers, stunned the simple faithful:

> I see that many times in the Church, over and above this case, but including this case, people search for "sins from youth," for example, and then publish them. . . . So much is written about the gay lobby. I still haven't found anyone with an identity card in the Vatican with "gay" on it. They say there are some there. I believe that when you are dealing with such a person, you must distinguish between the fact of a person being gay and the fact of someone forming a lobby, because not all lobbies are good. This one is not good. If someone is gay and is searching for the Lord and has good will, then *who am I to judge him*?[105]

By shifting from the issue of sinful homosexual relations, which was at the heart of the question, to same-sex attraction, which can be involuntary, the pope seemed to imply in his imprecise language that he judges neither same-sex

105. Pope Francis, "Apostolic Journey to Rio de Janeiro on the Occasion of the XXVIII World Youth Day—Press Conference of Pope Francis During the Return Flight—Papal Flight, Sunday, July 28, 2013," Vatican.va, https://www.vatican.va/content/francesco/en /speeches/2013/july/documents/papa-francesco_20130728_gmg-conferenza-stampa.html. (Our emphasis.)

attracted people nor those who engage in homosexual acts. That was how the media interpreted the phrase "Who am I to judge?" and trumpeted it throughout the world. There was no subsequent papal clarification.

This surprising attitude led the most important pro-homosexual monthly, *The Advocate*, to make Pope Francis their "Person of the Year." The publication justified its choice, saying, "Pope Francis's stark change in rhetoric from his two predecessors—both who were at one time or another among *The Advocate*'s annual Phobie Awards—makes what he's done in 2013 all the more daring."[106]

Then came Pope Francis's friendly encounters with homosexual pairs and transgender individuals, which scandalized the faithful. The most shocking of these, due to the contrasting attitudes, occurred during his 2015 visit to the United States. At the Apostolic Nunciature, he was introduced to Mrs. Kim Davis, the Clerk of Rowan County, Kentucky. She had spent six days in jail for refusing to register a homosexual "marriage," citing conscientious objection and her status as a Christian. The day before, the pope welcomed a former student named Yayo Grassi, who came with his homosexual partner, Iwan Bagus. The pontiff warmly embraced both partners in front of the cameras. The two encounters made media headlines for opposite reasons.

Fr. Federico Lombardi, then-Director of the Press Office of the Holy See, published a statement to clarify that the meeting with Mrs. Davis had been swift, among a group of people invited not by the pope but the Nunciature and, therefore, "his meeting with her should not be considered a form of support of her position in all of its particular and complex aspects."

---

106. Lucas Grindley, "The Advocate's Person of the Year: Pope Francis," *The Advocate*, Dec. 16, 2013, https://www.advocate.com/year-review/2013/12/16/advocates-person-year-pope-francis.

Instead, the statement emphasized, "the only real audience granted by the pope at the Nunciature was with one of his former students and his family."[107] What an eloquent display of double standards!

Already in January 2015, Pope Francis had received a Spanish transgender woman named Neria Lejárraga from Plasencia in an audience at his residence in Santa Marta. In a letter to the pope, she complained that the Catholics rejected her in her city after she had sex reassignment surgery and "married" another woman. The pope called her on the phone, invited her to the Vatican with all expenses paid by the Nunciature in Madrid, and received her in the company of her "fiancée."[108] In the following year, during his airplane interview returning from Georgia and Azerbaijan, the pontiff recounted in detail the circumstances of that meeting, constantly referring to Neria in the masculine ("he, who had been she, but is he") without any rebuke for the sex change surgery and subsequent "marriage" to another woman.[109]

Even more newsworthy was the official reception at the Apostolic Palace of Xavier Bettel, prime minister of Luxembourg, accompanied by his homosexual partner, the architect Gauthier Destenay, with whom he entered into a civil union in 2010 and then "married" in 2015 when the Grand Duchy legalized homosexual "marriage." The pretext was the

---

107. Holy See Press Office, "Statement Regarding a Meeting of Pope Francis and Mrs. Kim Davis at the Nunciature in Washington, D.C. (Fr. F. Lombardi, Director of the Press Office of the Holy See), Oct. 2, 2015, Vatican.va, https://press.vatican.va/content/sala stampa/it/bollettino/pubblico/2015/10/02/0749/01616.html.

108. See "El papa recibe en audiencia privada a un transexual español," *El País*, Jan. 27, 2015, http://politica.elpais.com/politica/2015/01/27/actualidad/1422355975_624238.html.

109. Pope Francis, "Apostolic Journey of His Holiness Pope Francis to Georgia and Azerbaijan (30 September – 2 October 2016)—In-Flight Press Conference of His Holiness Pope Francis From Azerbaijan to Rome—Papal Flight, Sunday, Oct. 2, 2016," Vatican.va, http://w2.vatican.va/content/francesco/pt/speeches/2016/october/documents /papa-francesco_20161002_georgia-azerbaijan-conferenza-stampa.html.

meeting of European leaders in the Eternal City to celebrate the 60th anniversary of the Treaty of Rome, which started what is now the European Union.[110] Pablo Iglesias, the leader of Spain's ultra-left Podemos party, immediately posted a photo of the papal reception on his Twitter account with the caption: "Xavier Bettel, prime minister of Luxembourg, received at the Vatican with his husband. And here [Cardinal] Cañizares says that gays go to hell." Bettel replied shortly afterward with another tweet: "It was a great pleasure and honor for me and Gauthier to be welcomed by the leader of the Catholic church."[111]

Pope Francis has often given special treatment to groups that advertise the homosexual agenda in the Church under the pretext of pastoral care for homosexuals and their parents when these groups organize pilgrimages to Rome and ask for tickets to attend the Wednesday general audiences. In these cases, they receive a much greater welcome than they expected.

In 2015, a pilgrimage group of forty-eight homosexual Catholics and supporters led by Sr. Jeannine Gramick received VIP seating at the papal audience in St. Peter's Square on Ash Wednesday. The nun had written the pope in advance, asking him to meet personally with the group. Two weeks before departure, she received a letter letting her know that tickets were reserved for the audience, and she assumed they were general seating tickets. On the day of the audience, papal ushers led them to the level of the Square where the pope sits. They were astonished![112]

110. See Cecilia Rodriguez, "Pope Francis' Welcome to World's Only Openly Gay Prime Minister Rekindles Vatican Controversy," *Forbes*, Apr. 9, 2017, https://www.forbes.com /sites/ceciliarodriguez/2017/04/09/pope-franciss-welcome-to-worlds-only-openly-gay -prime-minister-rekindles-vatican-controversy/#6cb67112a607.

111. "Pablo Iglesias cree que los obispos españoles no entenderían esta foto," Huffingtonpost.es, Mar. 25, 2017, http://www.huffingtonpost.es/2017/03/25/pablo -iglesias-obispos-foto_a_22011379/.

112. See Francis DeBernardo, "New Ways Ministry's LGBT Catholic Pilgrims Get VIP Seats

Four years later, also on Ash Wednesday, the English group called "LGBT+ Catholics Westminster Pastoral Council" from the archdiocese of Westminster (London) had the privilege of having their photo taken with the pope, who gave each of them a rosary as a gift. The pilgrimage organizer commented: "We were taken completely by surprise to be told that we were going to have our photograph taken with Pope Francis. Although we had asked Cardinal Vincent Nichols' office to obtain papal audience tickets for us, we certainly hadn't requested this—not even thought about it!" Another pilgrim, who had taken part in previous pilgrimages with the group, said: "This just keeps getting better and better!"[113]

During COVID-19, a parish priest from the Torvaianica district on the outskirts of Rome helped a group of Latin American transsexuals living in prostitution with money received from the Holy See's almshouse and at the pope's recommendation. Because of the lockdown, they found themselves in a precarious situation due to the lack of "clients." When the health restrictions were lifted, Pope Francis met with the group, the parish priest, and a nun on at least four occasions between April and August 2022 after the Wednesday papal audiences. The *Osservatore Romano* reported on the sequence of meetings.[114]

On the Catholic Church's World Day of the Poor in November 2023, Torvaianica's "trans" group was invited to join more than a thousand other poor and homeless people in the

at Papal Audience," New Ways Ministry, Feb. 19, 2015, https://www.newwaysministry. org/2015/02/19/new-ways-ministrys-lgbt-catholic-pilgrims-get-vip-seats-at-papal-audience/.

113. Robert Shine, "Pope Francis Meets With LGBT Pilgrims as Sixth Anniversary of His Election Approaches," New Ways Ministry, Mar. 12, 2019, https://www.newwaysministry .org/2019/03/12/pope-francis-meets-with-lgbt-pilgrims-as-sixth-anniversary-of-his -election-approaches/.

114. See Iacopo Scaramuzzi, "Pope Francis Has Met Regularly With Transgender Catholics at General Audiences," (trans. Massimo and Sarah Faggioli and Griffin Leynick), Outreach.faith, Jan. 13, 2023, https://outreach.faith/2023/01/pope-francis -meets-regularly-with-transgender-catholics-at-general-audience/.

Vatican auditorium for lunch as Pope Francis's guests. Some of the trans group members were placed at the table next to the sovereign pontiff.[115]

However, the most shocking thing for Catholic defenders of traditional marriage and the family have been the letters Pope Francis sent to Church figures with heterodox positions and the friendly meetings he has had with some of them at Casa Santa Marta.

In August 2015, lesbian writer Francesca Pardi, author of *Piccolo uovo* (Little Egg)—a children's book whose characters are same-sex attracted penguins, lesbian rabbits, a couple of mixed-breed dogs, and kangaroos who adopt polar bears— wrote to the Vatican after the mayor of Venice banned her book. She sent it to the pope, complaining about the "obscurantist" behavior of some Catholic associations and asking for the Church's support. She received a letter back from a Holy See official saying that "His Holiness is grateful for your delicate gesture and the sentiments that prompted it" and "looks forward to an increasingly fruitful activity in the service of younger generations and the spread of authentic human and Christian values," imparting the apostolic blessing. In the face of the scandal, the deputy director of the Vatican press office felt obliged to explain that "it was a private response and therefore not intended for publication (which unfortunately happened)" and that "The pope's blessing in the letter's closing is to the person and not to any teachings not in line with Church doctrine on gender theory."[116]

---

115. See Nicole Winfield and Trisha Thomas, "For This Group of Trans Women, the Pope and His Message of Inclusivity Are a Welcome Change," *Associated Press*, Nov. 19, 2023, https://apnews.com/article/vatican-transgender-lgbtq-b3d67868504ba701cce09da9ecc94de0.

116. "L'autrice dei libri gender scrive a Papa Francesco e lui risponde con una lettera," *Il Fatto Quotidiano*, Aug. 28, 2015, https://www.ilfattoquotidiano.it/2015/08/28/il-papa-benedice-lautrice-dei-libri-gender-messi-al-bando-dal-sindaco-di-venezia/1989845/.

While this episode was restricted to Italy, Pope Francis's glowing tributes to Fr. James Martin and Sr. Jeannine Gramick for their work with the homosexual community had worldwide repercussions. They were sent despite both openly dissenting from traditional Church teaching. The nun's case is severe because, under Pope John Paul II, the Holy See forbade her to continue this apostolate.

In April 2017, Pope Francis appointed Fr. James Martin as a consultant to the Holy See's Secretariat for Communications.[117] In the following years, the pope answered one of the latter's interviews and sent him three handwritten letters in Spanish to support his *Outreach* initiative, a website hosted on the servers of *America* magazine (The official publication of the Society of Jesus in the U.S.), to provide material to homosexual Catholics.

On the eve of an *Outreach* online conference in June 2021, Pope Francis thanked Father Martin for his "pastoral zeal," for imitating the "style of God," and offered prayers "for your faithful, your 'parishioners.'"[118] In 2022, after receiving a copy of the program for the second conference, he wrote again, asking him to continue working "in the culture of encounter, which shortens the distances and enriches us with differences."[119] In May 2023, he again sent his greetings to the participants of the conference to be held at Fordham Jesuit University the following month:

> Thank you for all the good you are doing. Thank you!
> I pray for you, please do so for me.

---

117. See Carol Glatz, "Pope Names 13 Consultors to Vatican Secretariat for Communications," *Catholic News Service*, Apr. 12, 2017, https://www.ncronline.org/pope-names-13-consultors-vatican-secretariat-communications.

118. Gerard O'Connell, "Pope Francis Encourages Jesuit Father James Martin in his L.G.B.T. Ministry," *America*, Jun. 27, 2021, https://www.americamagazine.org/faith/2021/06/27/james-martin-lgbt-ministry-pope-francis-240938.

119. Lisa Zengarini, "Pope to Jesuit Fr. Martin: 'Jesus Is Close to Everyone,'" *Vatican News*, Aug. 3, 2022, https://www.vaticannews.va/en/pope/news/2022-08/pope-to-father-martin-jesus-is-close-to-everyone.html.

I send my best regards to the members of the meeting at Fordham University. Thank you for delivering it to them. In my prayers and good wishes are you and all who are working at the Outreach Conference.

Again, thank you, thank you for your witness.[120]

In the short interview just before the second conference, the pope answered questions from Father Martin in writing on May 8, 2022. *Outreach* asked: "What would you say is the most important thing for LGBT people to know about God?" The pope answered: "God is Father and he does not disown any of his children. And 'the style' of God is 'closeness, mercy and tenderness.' Along this path you will find God."[121]

Encouraged by this support, Father Martin did not hesitate to correct the pope. On January 24, 2023, before his trip to Africa, where homosexual relations are outlawed Pope Francis was interviewed by Nicole Winfield of the Associated Press. Regarding homosexuality, he stated:

It's not a crime. Yes, but it's a sin. Fine, but first let's distinguish between a sin and a crime.

It's also a sin to lack charity with one another.[122]

Father Martin expressed bewilderment and asked for clarification. In a long handwritten note, which the Jesuit hastened to publish on his website, Pope Francis wrote:

It is not the first time that I speak of homosexuality and homosexual persons.

120. Outreach.faith, "Pope Francis Sends Greetings to This Year's Outreach Conference for LGBT Catholics," Outreach.faith, Jun. 14, 2023, https://outreach.faith/2023/06 /pope-francis-sends-greetings-to-this-years-outreach-conference-for-lgbtq-catholics/.

121. James Martin, "A Mini-Interview With the Holy Father," Outreach.faith, May 9, 2022, https://outreach.faith/2022/05/pope-francis-speaks-to-lgbtq-catholics/.

122. Nicole Winfield, "The AP Interview: Pope Says Homosexuality Not a Crime," *Associated Press*, Jan. 25, 2023, https://apnews.com/article/pope-francis-gay-rights-ap -interview-1359756ae22f27f87c1d4d6b9c8ce212.

And I wanted to clarify that it is not a crime in order to stress that criminalization is neither good nor just.

When I said it is a sin, I was simply referring to Catholic moral teaching, which says that *every sexual act outside of marriage is a sin.*[123]

To further express his support for Father Martin, Pope Francis granted him two private audiences in his library in Santa Marta. The first was a thirty-minute meeting on September 30, 2019. On that occasion, Father Martin said: "'I shared with Pope Francis the experiences of L.G.B.T. Catholics around the world, their joys and their hopes, their griefs and concerns. I also spoke about my own ministry to them and how they feel excluded.' He concluded then, 'I saw this audience as a sign of the Holy Father's care for L.G.B.T. people.'" The second audience was on November 11, 2022, and lasted forty-five minutes. According to Father Martin, it was "punctuated with a lot of laughter. It was very warm, very inspiring, and very encouraging." The pope "was incredibly supportive of me," Father Martin told *America's* correspondent in Rome.[124]

Pope Francis adopted the same encouraging attitudes toward Sr. Jeannine Gramick and *New Ways Ministry*. It is worth remembering that in May 1999, Cardinal Joseph Ratzinger notified the Congregation for the Doctrine of the Faith that the founders of *New Ways Ministry*, Fr. Robert Nugent and Sr. Jeannine Gramick, were forbidden to do pastoral work with homosexuals because of the "ambiguities and errors" of their approach. The organization was also officially criticized in

---

123. Outreach.faith, "Pope Francis Clarifies Comments on Homosexuality: 'One Must Consider the Circumstances,'" Outreach.faith, Jan. 27, 2023, https://outreach.faith/2023 /01/pope-francis-clarifies-comments-on-homosexuality-one-must-consider-the-circumstances/.

124. Gerard O'Connell, "Pope Francis Received Father James Martin in Private Audience for the Second Time," *America*, Nov. 1, 2022, https://www.americamagazine.org/faith /2022/11/11/james-martin-pope-francis-244131.

2010 by the U.S. Conference of Catholic Bishops for its public support of civil "marriage" for same-sex partners.

Pope Francis ignored these condemnations and fully welcomed both activists. We already reported on his 2015 VIP reception of the organization's group of pilgrims. Worse still, approaching the fiftieth anniversary of the founding of *New Ways Ministry*, on April 21, 2021, Francis DeBernardo, its executive director, wrote Pope Francis with an account of the organization's past. The pope replied on May 3, acknowledging that *New Ways Ministry's* "history has not been an easy one," but that "your letter, as it narrates with objectivity its history, gives me light to better understand certain situations," possibly an allusion to the condemnations. In a second letter, handwritten and dated June 17, Pope Francis thanked DeBernardo for his "heart, open to [his] neighbor." He also sent his cordial greetings to Sr. Jeannine Gramick, adding, "I know how much she has suffered. She is a valiant woman who makes her decisions in prayer."[125]

"The Holy Father's warm letter to *New Ways Ministry* is not only another step in his outreach to LGBTQ people, but the beginning of a kind of rehabilitation for *New Ways*, and for [*New Ways* cofounder] Sister Jeannine [Gramick] as well, in recognition of their important ministry in our church," Jesuit Fr. James Martin commented gleefully.[126]

On December 10, 2021, Pope Francis wrote a handwritten letter directly to Sr. Jeannine Gramick for the fiftieth anniversary of *New Ways Ministry*. The pope wrote:

---

125. Brian Fraga, "Pope Francis Thanks New Ways Ministry in Recent Correspondence," *National Catholic Reporter*, Dec. 8, 2021, https://www.ncronline.org/news/people/pope -francis-thanks-new-ways-ministry-recent-correspondence.

126. Robert Shine, "Pope Francis Writes to New Ways Ministry: 'Thank You for Your Neighborly Work,'" New Ways Ministry, Dec. 9, 2021, https://www.newwaysministry.org /2021/12/09/pope-francis-writes-to-new-ways-ministry-thank-you-for-your-neighborly -work/.

"You have not been afraid of 'closeness' [with homosexuals] and in getting close you did it 'feeling the pain' and without condemning anyone, but with the 'tenderness' of a sister and a mother."

"Thank you, Sr. Jeannine," the letter concluded, "for all your closeness, compassion and tenderness."[127]

Sr. Gramick told *America* magazine, the first press outlet to report on the letter, that many Catholics will read the arrival of these letters to *New Ways Ministry* as an institutional affirmation of their work. Invigorated by that support, she wants the Church to make even more significant progress in achieving the goals of the homosexual agenda. In an interview published by *America* the same day the pope's letter was released, Sr. Gramick stated:

> Gay people say to me, "Pope Francis is wonderful, but he hasn't changed the teaching of the church." Well, that is not his job right now. Eventually, it's his job, but right now it's up to us, the people, to articulate the faith. . . .
>
> We have to stand up for what we believe in . . . . We have to follow our consciences. We need people in the pews to start writing letters to their bishops saying they are withdrawing donations until you start treating L.G.B.T. people as human beings and stop ostracizing them because you're hurting not only them but the whole body of Christ.
>
> Sometimes we have to go against what the leaders of our church say.[128]

As if this epistolary support was not enough, Pope Francis wanted to go further. On October 17, 2023, as the assembly

---

127. Jim McDermott, "Pope Francis Praises Sister Jeannine Gramick's 50 Years of L.G.B.T. Ministry in Handwritten Letter," *America*, Jan. 7, 2022, https://www.americamagazine.org /faith/2022/01/07/sister-jeanine-gramick-letter-pope-francis-242157.

128. Jim McDermott, "Interview: Sister Jeannine Gramick on Being Censured by the Vatican, 50 Years of Ministry and Her Hopes for LGBT Catholics," *America*, Jan. 7, 2022, https://www.americamagazine.org/faith/2022/01/07/sister-jeanine-gramick-new -ways-ministry-242155.

of the Synod of Bishops on Synodality was in session in the Paul VI Hall, and small groups were discussing the question of fully accepting homosexual partners in the Church, Pope Francis received a delegation from *New Ways Ministry* led by Sr. Jeannine Gramick. He gave them a 50-minute audience at his Santa Marta residence. After the meeting, the association said it "is remarkable because it reflects the steady acceptance of Catholic officials to LGBTQ+ issues and ministry. Previous popes and church leaders have opposed Sister Jeannine and *New Ways Ministry*. This meeting now represents a new openness to the pastorally-motivated, justice-seeking approach which Sister Jeannine and her organization have long practiced."[129]

In an interview with the Italian portal *Open*, and revealing a modernist conception of the evolution of dogma, Sr. Jeannine Gramick predicted that the Church would eventually recognize homosexual "marriage": "'It is not a pope's task to change the Church's teaching. The pontiff must proclaim the people's faith. He can make an official pronouncement only when he knows what the people believe. As in the early Church, people must come together, speak from their own experiences and listen to them.' So, the Church will eventually approve gay marriage: 'One day it will, but this is just my opinion. The people of God must confront this issue in future synods.'"[130]

---

129. Robert Shine, "Pope Francis Receives Sr. Jeannine Gramick at Vatican," New Ways Ministry, Oct. 17, 2023, https://www.newwaysministry.org/2023/10/17/pope-francis-receives-sr-jeannine-gramick-at-vatican/.

130. "La suora ribelle riabilitata da Papa Francesco: 'Nella Chiesa del futuro matrimoni gay e donne cardnale,'" Open.Online, Oct. 23, 2023, https://www.open.online/2023/10/23/jeannine-gramick-suora-papa-francesco-matrimoni-gay/.

CHAPTER 9

Attempting to Change Church Doctrine at the Synod Under the Pretext of "Radical Inclusion"

The dominant progressive current in the German hierarchy immediately went through the floodgate opened by Pope Francis's stance. Under the pretext of eliminating the causes of priestly sexual abuse of minors, the German bishops, complicit with the country's largest organization of lay Catholics, the Central Committee of German Catholics (ZdK), embarked on a disastrous "synodal way" to change the Catholic Church's hierarchical structure and moral teachings.

One of the German Synodal Way's official documents stated:

Same-sex sexuality—also realized in sexual acts—is therefore not a sin that separates from God, and is not to be judged as intrinsically evil. . . .

1. . . . passages 2357–2359 and 2396 (homosexuality and chastity) of the *Catechism* [*of the Catholic Church*] should be revised as part of a necessary re-evaluation of homosexuality. . . . "Homosexual acts" must be removed from the list of "grave sins against chastity" in the *Catechism*.[131]

The German Synodal Way's heretical proposals on sexual morality, female priesthood, and the Church's hierarchical structure aroused much opposition in various episcopates. Despite that controversial climate, Pope Francis decided to convene a two-year synod on synodality, the preparation for

---

131. Der Synodale Weg, *Handlungstext: Lehramtliche Neubewertung von Homosexualität*, p. 5, accessed Apr. 21, 2024, https://www.synodalerweg.de/fileadmin/Synodalerweg/Dokumente _Reden_Beitraege/beschluesse-broschueren/SW8-Handlungstext_Lehramtliche NeubewertungvonHomosexualitaet_2022.pdf.

which also served as a platform for advancing the demands of the homosexual movement in the Church.

The fallacy used was that a synodal Church should listen to the People of God to find out what the Holy Spirit is saying through the signs of the times. If the Catholic base showed openness to the homosexual agenda, they could conclude that the Church's traditional teachings are no longer valid because they are no longer accepted and practiced by the laity, the faithful interpreters of the Holy Spirit.

For this listening exercise, they organized discussion sessions around questionnaires sent by the Secretariat of the Synod of Bishops. These preparatory documents raised the same issues under discussion in the German Synodal Way. They urged parishes to incorporate *marginalized* people into the discussions, including individuals in extramarital or adulterous unions and homosexuals. Of course, groups of Catholic homosexuals rushed to send representatives to as many parishes as possible to influence the discussions.

The Synod Secretariat also opened a website to receive submissions from Catholic groups, which the homosexual movement used to advertise their ideas. The most significant instance was that the official website published a drawing of a group of young people holding hands and raising their arms, in a somewhat vindicative attitude of celebration, around a homosexual Pride activist flanked by a girl in priestly vestments.

On the documentary section of the same website, *New Ways Ministry* posted a link to a video encouraging its members to attend the Synod. However, an official aware of the past condemnations of the association by the Vatican and the U.S. Bishops' Conference removed the link. As the association protested, the Synod communications director reinstated the video and sent an apology "to all LGBT [people] and to the members of *New Ways Ministries* for the pain caused." The association warmly accepted what it called the Church's "historic" admission of "the harm that such a slight would have caused LGBTQ people and the entire church."[132]

Unsurprisingly, given this participation and pressure from above, many parish reports and national summaries mentioned the need to fully welcome homosexuals. In many cases, there were formal requests that the Church change its doctrine by accepting all those who "love each other" and live together conjugally without being married: cohabiting, domestic, or life partners; divorced and civilly "remarried" individuals; and homosexuals.

Media headlines reported that these demands had been taken up in national reports: "Luxembourg Synod Calls for 'Gay Marriage,'"[133] "Italian Catholics Call for More Attention to LGBTQ People,"[134] "In Synod Reports, US Catholics Call for Women's Leadership, LGBTQ Welcoming,"[135] "Spanish Archdioceses Want an End to Celibacy, Women's Ordination, and Acceptance of Same-Sex Unions."[136] A jubilant *Cristianos Gay* website republished a title of the Jesuit Vale dos Sinos

132. Nicole Winfield, "Vatican Apologizes for Removing Catholic LGBT Advocacy Group From Synod Website," *America*, Dec. 13, 2021, https://www.americamagazine.org/politics -society/2021/12/13/vatican-new-ways-ministry-synod-242024.

133. Luke Coppen, "Luxembourg Synod Calls for 'Gay Marriage,'" *The Catholic Thing*, Jul. 28, 2022, https://www.thecatholicthing.org/2022/07/28/luxembourg-synod-calls -for-gay-marriage/.

134. "I cattolici italiani chiedono più attenzione per le persone Lgbtq," Open.Online, Aug. 18, 2022, https://www.open.online/2022/08/18/cattolici-italiani-accoglienza-persone-lgbtq/.

135. Brian Fraga, "In Synod Reports, US Catholics Call for Women's Leadership, LGBTQ Welcoming," *National Catholic Reporter*, Aug. 16, 2022, https://www.ncronline.org/news /synod-reports-us-catholics-call-womens-leadership-lgbtq-welcoming.

136. "Arquidioceses espanholas querem fim do celibato, ordenação de mulheres e aceitação de uniões do mesmo sexo," ACIDigital, Jun. 7, 2022, https://www.acidigital.com/noticia /52312/arquidioceses-espanholas-querem-fim-do-celibato-ordenacao-de-mulheres-e- aceitacao-de-unioes-do-mesmo-sexo.

University's online magazine: "As the Global Synod Progresses, LGBTQ+ Inclusion Is a Prominent Theme in Country Reports."[137]

Ahead of the Synod's continental stage, its Secretariat presented a working document intended to synthesize the national reports under the suggestive title "Enlarge the Space of Your Tent." A section titled "Listening That Becomes Welcoming" referred to those who, in the previous stage, had felt "a tension between belonging to the Church and their own loving relationships, such as: remarried divorcees, single parents, people living in a polygamous marriage, LGBTQ people, etc."[138]

The same document suggested a "radical inclusion" of all those who felt marginalized. In an article for the Jesuit *America* magazine, Cardinal Robert McElroy, bishop of San Diego, was quick to explain this phrase and point out its sacramental consequences. In opposition to Saint Paul (see 1 Cor. 11:27, 29), he proposed that divorced and remarried Catholics or homosexuals seeking God's grace in their lives should not be categorically excluded from receiving Holy Communion at Mass.[139] He was quickly rebuked by Most Rev. Thomas Paprocki, bishop of Springfield, Illinois, former chairman of the Canon Law Committee of the U.S. Conference of Catholic Bishops, who, without quoting him by name, wrote an article in *First Things* titled: "Imagining a Heretical Cardinal."[140]

---

137. "A medida que avanza el Sínodo Global, la inclusión LGBTQ+ es un tema destacado en los informes nacionales," CristianosGays.com, Aug. 27, 2022, https://www.cristianosgays .com/2022/08/27/a-medida-que-avanza-el-sinodo-global-la-inclusion-lgbtq-es-un-tema -destacado-en-los-informes-nacionales/.

138. Secretaria Generalis Synodi, "Enlarge the Space of Your Tent"—Working Document for the Continental Stage (Oct. 24, 2022), Synod.va, no. 39, p. 18, https://www.synod.va /content/dam/synod/common/phases/continental-stage/dcs/20221025-ENG-DTC-FINAL -OK.pdf.

139. See Robert W. McElroy, "Cardinal McElroy on 'Radical Inclusion' for L.G.B.T. People, Women and Others in the Catholic Church," *America*, Jan. 24, 2023, https:// www.americamagazine.org/faith/2023/01/24/mcelroy-synodality-inclusion-244587.

140. Thomas J. Paprocki, "Imagining a Heretical Cardinal," *First Things*, Feb. 28, 2023, https://www.firstthings.com/web-exclusives/2023/02/imagining-a-heretical-cardinal.

Seeking to advance this radical welcoming agenda, Cardinal Jean-Claude Hollerich, archbishop of Luxembourg, the Synod on Synodality's General Rapporteur, stated in an interview for the Vatican website, "Everyone is called. No one is excluded: even remarried divorcees, even homosexuals, everyone. The kingdom of God is not an exclusive club. It opens its doors to everyone without discrimination."[141]

After receiving the reports of the Continental Stage sessions, the Synod Secretariat prepared an *Instrumentum Laboris* with a series of statements and questions to be debated during the Plenary Session in the Vatican. This working document further thickened the witches' brew. "The Final Documents of the Continental Assemblies often mention those who do not feel accepted in the Church, such as the divorced and re-married, people in polygamous marriages or LGBTQ+ people."

This led to the question: "How can we create spaces where those who feel hurt by the Church and unwelcomed by the community feel recognized, received, free to ask questions and not [be] judged? In the light of the post-synodal apostolic exhortation *Amoris laetitia*, what concrete steps are needed to welcome those who feel excluded from the Church because of their status or sexuality (for example, remarried divorcees, people in polygamous marriages, LGBTQ+ people, etc.)?"[142]

To guide the debates toward this openness, Pope Francis invited the Dominican Friar Timothy Radcliffe to preach a retreat to the Plenary Assembly of the Synod participants on

---

141. "Relator do Sínodo da Sinodalidade defende uniões homossexuais e de divorciados em entrevista a site da Santa Sé," ACIDigital, Oct. 26, 2022, https://www.acidigital.com /noticia/53606/relator-do-sinodo-da-sinodalidade-defende-unioes-homossexuais-e-de -divorciados-em-entrevista-a-site-da-santa-se.

142. "XVI Ordinary General Assembly of the Synod of Bishops for a Synodal Church: Communion, Participation, Mission—Instrumentum Laboris—For the First Session— (October 2023)" (Jun. 20, 2023), Vatican.va, https://press.vatican.va/content/sala stampa/it/bollettino/pubblico/2023/06/20/0456/01015.html#en.

the eve of its inauguration. Father Radcliffe had made a name for himself during his time as his order's Master General for accepting novices with an ingrained homosexual tendency, contrary to the instructions of the Holy See. Further, he scandalized conservative Anglicans with his contribution to the so-called Pilling Report (on human sexuality) by a working group of Anglican bishops, which served as the basis for the partial approval of homosexual religious "marriage" in the Church of England.

In this Report's second section dealing with the ethical issues of homosexual practices, Father Radcliffe did not hesitate to blaspheme, writing that, when considering same-sex relationships, "we cannot begin with the question of whether it is permitted or forbidden! We must ask what it means and how far it is Eucharistic. Certainly it can be generous, vulnerable, tender, mutual and nonviolent. So in many ways, I think it can be expressive of Christ's self-gift."[143]

In addition to preaching the retreat, Father Radcliffe gave spiritual reflections at the beginning of each weekly session. In the last one, recalling that a Canadian girl triggered sympathy when reporting her sister's suicide, the Dominican emphasized, "Many of us wept when we heard of that young woman who committed suicide because she was bisexual and did not feel welcomed in the Church. I hope it changed us. The Holy Father reminded us that all are welcome."[144]

Despite this emotional pressure, to the dismay of Fr. James Martin and other militants of "building bridges" with the homo-

---

143. Joan Frawley Desmond, "Father Timothy Radcliffe's Designation as Synod on Synodality's Retreat Master Stirs Anxiety," *National Catholic Register*, Jan. 27, 2023, https://www.ncregister.com/news/father-timothy-radcliffe-s-designation-as-synod-on -synodality-s-retreat-master-stirs-anxiety.

144. Colm Flynn, "Synod on Synodality Report," EWTN News Nightly, Oct. 19, 2023, https://www.ewtnvatican.com/articles/synod-on-synodality-report-1711.

sexual movement, the Final Document of the first session did not address the theme of welcoming homosexuals, nor did it use the L.G.B.T. acronym, thanks to the opposition of many Synod Fathers and particularly the delegations of bishops from Africa.

This internal resistance in the Synod's Plenary Assembly to the advance of the homosexual agenda did not prevent Pope Francis and Cardinal Fernández, a month and a half later, from publishing the declaration *Fiducia supplicans* in a very non-synodal manner, and without even consulting the other members of the Dicastery for the Doctrine of the Faith.

CHAPTER 10

Blessing Homosexual Partnerships, a First Step Toward "Radical Inclusion"

In the culture war to normalize homosexuality, symbolic facts are as important as the spreading of ideas, perhaps even more so, because they mobilize people's emotions and feelings, which today matter more than principles for much of public opinion.

One of the first concessional gestures the homosexual movement had to secure from the Catholic Church was to have priests—her representatives—bless homosexual pairs who came before them. For example, since its founding in 1991, the Christian Association of Lesbians, Gays, Transsexuals, and Bisexuals of Catalonia (A.C.G.I.L.) has put several homosexual pairs a year in contact with "5 or 6 priests of trust" who are willing to bless their union, in a ceremony that is always done "with the utmost discretion," "without photos or any kind of public," either in the partners' home or in the priest's own church.[145]

In Germany, the spokesman for the Community of Homosexuals and the Church told *Der Spiegel* magazine there are ceremonies where homosexual pairs come secretly, only with friends, siblings, or parents, to receive a blessing and occasionally exchange rings in the traditional way. Describing one such ceremony that took place in Cologne, he said, "It was like a bridal mass with about thirty people, a ring blessing, and classic wedding rituals" while the organ played "Great God, we praise you."[146]

The same thing has happened for decades in practically every country having associations of homosexuals who declare themselves Catholic and priests who act as chaplains

---

145. "Bendición clandestina de parejas LGTBI: una organización une a sacerdotes y parejas," *El Confidencial*, Jul. 1, 2021, https://www.elconfidencial.com/espana/2021-07 -01/sacerdotes-catalanes-bendicen-clandestino-parejas-homosexuales_3161276/.

146. "Riskanter Segen für gleichgeschlechtliche Paare," *Spiegel*, Aug. 9, 2003, https:// www.spiegel.de/spiegel/vorab/a-260660.html.

for them. Sometimes, they did not hold a formal ceremony, even if private, but an informal blessing of the pair during a home visit, as Gery Kezler, the organizer of Vienna's Life Ball, Europe's largest AIDS fundraising event, revealed in an interview with Austrian television. On August 15, the feast of the Assumption, in 2018, he invited a group of friends to have lunch at his country home, and on this occasion, Cardinal Christoph Schönborn, archbishop of Vienna, blessed him and his partner after the meal. Then they opened a bottle of champagne, and the cork broke a valuable Meissen porcelain plate.[147] Cardinal Schönborn's complicity with the homosexual pair had begun nine months earlier when they jointly organized a performance by the Drag Queen Thomas Neuwirth (stage name Conchita Wurst) in St. Stephen's Cathedral, an event in memory of AIDS victims.[148]

However, the homosexual movement was not satisfied with private ceremonies. It had to start organizing public blessing rituals. The best opportunity for that was St. Valentine's feast day, as many parishes organized Masses followed by the blessing of engaged and married couples. Homosexual pairs could easily present themselves at Mass and line up with others to receive the blessing. In addition, the Vienna cathedral served as an incentive since an Austrian public television program filmed one of these events, and the cathedral rector earned public thanks from a homosexual pair.[149]

147. See Novus Ordo Watch, "Austrian Homo Activist Says 'Cardinal' Schonborn Blessed His Relationship," YouTube.com, Novus Ordo Watch channel, Sept. 19, 2018, accessed Apr. 18, 2024, https://www.youtube.com/watch?v=oV-g8aR01Sg.

148. See Christa Pongratz-Lippitt, "Cardinal Leads First-Ever AIDS Day Requiem in Vienna Cathedral," La Croix, Dec. 4, 2017, https://international.la-croix.com/news/culture /cardinal-leads-first-ever-aids-day-requiem-in-vienna-cathedral/6492. See also, Wikipedia contributors, "Conchita Wurst," Wikipedia, The Free Encyclopedia, accessed Apr. 26, 2024, https://en.wikipedia.org/w/index.php?title=Conchita_Wurst&oldid=1219830117.

149. See Josef Wallner, "Mehr als ein normaler Segen," Kirchenzeitung.at, Apr. 28, 2020, https://www.kirchenzeitung.at/site/themen/gesellschaftsoziales/mehr-als-ein-normaler-segen.

Gradually, the priests promoting such blessing ceremonies gave them more publicity, especially in Germany, Austria, and Switzerland. One of the most scandalous cases was that of Fr. Christoph Simonsen. In 2003, he organized five blessing ceremonies for homosexual pairs before three hundred attendees at his Maria Hilf (Mary Help of Christians) church in Mönchengladbach, diocese of Aachen, during a Liturgy of the Word with prayers and biblical readings while the homosexual pair sat in the front row. Explaining his activities to the diocesan presbyteral council, Father Simonsen said that "strengthening established same-sex partnerships" had a "liberating power."[150]

Perhaps the most headline-grabbing case occurred in February 2021 in Pope Francis's native Argentina. In the Patagonian city of Ushuaia, a Salesian parish priest celebrated, "during a religious ceremony that included all the traditional components of Catholic worship," the union between the Secretary of Education and the Undersecretary for Diversity of the Tierra del Fuego province. The latter government official is a transsexual who presents himself as a woman. In attendance were the provincial governor and various of his cabinet members, as well as the former governor during whose term in office the first homosexual civil "marriage" in Latin America was celebrated in 2009. During the ceremony, "they read the Gospel, the spouses promised fidelity, they recited the Our Father and the Hail Mary, and the bride and groom and many of the sixty parishioners present received Communion."[151] The transsexual in the role of the bride stated: "We talked to Father Fabian with the idea of doing this ceremony, and he

---

150. "Riskanter Segen für gleichgeschlechtliche Paare."

151. "Un hombre y una mujer trans se casaron por iglesia en Ushuaia con todos los ritos del catolicismo," *La Voz*, Feb. 6, 2021, https://www.lavoz.com.ar/ciudadanos/un-hombre-y-una-mujer-trans-se-casaron-por-iglesia-en-ushuaia-con-todos-ritos-del-catolic/.

accepted. He told us that he only evaluates people's capacity to love. Of course, he consulted with the diocese."[152]

In a later statement, the bishop limited himself to saying that "this diocese did not authorize this celebration" and that "the priest in question has already been suitably warned." He added, "While accompanying all persons without exception in their legitimate desire to receive God's blessing, we wish to point out that, in this case, we are not dealing with the sacrament of marriage as the Church believes and holds."[153] Who was this bishop? It was Most Rev. Jorge Ignacio García Cuerva, whom Pope Francis later promoted to archbishop of Buenos Aires and primate of Argentina.

Priests who openly violated canonical provisions and the rules established in documents of the Holy See were rarely punished. The most eloquent case was that of Maltese Dominican Fr. Mark Montebello, who, in 2015, blessed rings during a private engagement ceremony for two known homosexuals. A photo of the episode was posted to Facebook, prompting a report in Malta's leading newspaper and a great deal of controversy. Immediately, however, a Facebook group was formed in support of the priest. The archbishop, Most Rev. Charles Scicluna, and the superior of the Dominican friars on the island summoned the offender to a meeting, after which he received no sanction. In a statement, the archdiocese affirmed:

> During the cordial meeting, the archbishop encouraged Fr. Mark to continue his outreach to gay people and requested that he continue to follow Church practice and discipline in his ministry, especially in the celebration of sacred rites and Church rituals.

152. "'Ni perder la fe ni dejar de ser hija de Dios,'" *Rueda de Prensa*, Feb. 8, 2021 https://ruedadeprensa.com.ar/2021/02/08/ni-perder-la-fe-ni-dejar-de-ser-hija-de-dios/.

153. "El obispo de Río Gallegos dice que no autorizó la ceremonia ni hubo matrimonio en la profanación oficiada por un salesiano," InfoCatólica, Feb. 9, 2021, https://www.infocatolica.com/?t=noticia&cod=39795.

Fr. Mark thanked the archbishop and the vicar general for their support and agreed that in his pastoral ministry to gay people, he would continue to follow Church practices and discipline.[154]

This impunity encouraged the progressive sector in the Church to defend the need for official acceptance of these blessing ceremonies and the preparation of a specific ritual for homosexual unions. This pressure was particularly intense in Austria and Germany.

In 2015, during the Synod on the Family, the Central Committee of German Catholics (ZdK) proposed "a further development of liturgical forms, in particular blessings of same-sex partnerships, new partnerships of the divorced, and for important decisions in family life."[155] Several German bishops later reiterated this proposal. In January 2018, Most Rev. Franz-Josef Bode, bishop of Osnabrück, said in an interview with German journalists that blessing same-sex unions was possible in German Catholic churches.[156] The following month, Cardinal Reinhard Marx, archbishop of Munich and Freising, then-president of the German Bishops' Conference, hinted in an interview that such blessings were possible.[157]

The following year, the prestigious Herder publishing house released the book *Mit Dem Segen Der Kirche?:*

---

154. Robert Shine, "Priest Blesses Same-Gender Couple's Engagement in Malta; Archbishop Remains Calm," New Ways Ministry, Apr. 15, 2015, https://www.newways ministry.org/2015/04/15/priest-blesses-same-gender-couples-engagement-in-malta -archbishop-remains-calm/.

155. ZdK, "Zwischen Lehre und Lebenswelt Brücken bauen—Familie und Kirche in der Welt von heute," ZdK.de, accessed Apr. 19, 2024, https://www.zdk.de/veroeffentlichungen /erklaerungen/detail/Zwischen-Lehre-und-Lebenswelt-Bruecken-bauen-Familie-und -Kirche-in-der-Welt-von-heute-225w/.

156. See "Bischof Bode für Segnung von Homo-Paaren," NDR.de, Jan. 10, 2018, https:// web.archive.org/web/20180110181002/https://www.ndr.de/nachrichten/niedersachsen /Bischof-Bode-fuer-Segnung-von-Homo-Paaren,segnung100.html.

157. See "Kardinal Marx und die Segnung von Homo-Paaren," Katholisches.info, Feb. 5, 2018, https://katholisches.info/2018/02/05/kardinal-marx-und-die-segnung-von-homo-paaren/.

Gleichgeschlechtliche Partnerschaft Im Fokus Der Pastoral ("With the Church's Blessing? Same-Sex Unions in the Focus of Pastoral Care") under the direction of Stephan Loos, Michael Reitemeyer, and Georg Trettin with a foreword by Most Rev. Franz-Josef Bode, bishop of Osnabrück, and Most Rev. Stefan Hesse, archbishop of Hamburg. It also included an anthology of lectures given at a symposium of the Academy of the Diocese of Osnabrück on the possibility of blessing ceremonies for homosexual unions. According to Loos, options within canon law already exist: "Under certain conditions, a local bishop may issue norms for the liturgy, which may also include blessings."[158]

In 2020, the Liturgical Commission of the Austrian Bishops' Conference, chaired by Most Rev. Franz Lackner, archbishop of Salzburg, asked liturgical theologians Fr. Ewald Volgger and Florian Wegscheider to compile a study with contributions from various specialists on the possibility of giving homosexual unions an official blessing. The result was the work *Benediktion von gleichgeschlechtlichen Partnerschaften* ["Blessing of Same-Sex Partnerships"], published by the Catholic University of Linz. The book's first half deals with same-sex "marriages" in Austria from an ethical and biblical point of view. The second half deals with liturgical aspects and offers suggestions for blessing rituals.[159]

Given the spread of public ceremonies blessing homosexual partners, as well as studies and statements favoring them, a bishop sent the Congregation for the Doctrine of the Faith a query, in the form of a *dubium*, regarding the lawfulness

---

158. Christoph Paul Hartmann, "Ist ein Segen für homosexuelle Paare möglich?" Katholisch.de, Aug. 29, 2019, https://www.katholisch.de/artikel/22758-ist-ein-segen-fuer-homosexuelle-paare-moeglich.

159. See Christa Pongratz-Lippitt, "New Book Charts Path to Same-Sex Benedictions," *The Tablet*, May 6, 2020, https://www.thetablet.co.uk/news/12869/new-book-charts-path-to-same-sex-benedictions.

of such blessings. After studying the question in detail, on March 15, 2021, the Congregation published the *Responsum* mentioned in the first chapter, which essentially says that the Church does not have the power to bless same-sex unions since what is blessed must be objectively and positively in accordance with God's designs.[160] Both the Congregation's prefect, Cardinal Luis Ladaria, and the secretary, Archbishop Giacomo Morandi, signed the *Responsum*.

At the Angelus the following Sunday, Pope Francis spoke twice of God's style being one of "closeness, compassion, and tenderness," which must be sown "not with theoretical condemnations but with gestures of love," overcoming "misunderstandings, difficulty, or persecution, or claims of legalism, or clerical moralism."[161] According to *America*'s correspondent in Rome, well-informed Vatican sources interpreted these words of the pope as an allusion to the Congregation for the Doctrine of the Faith statement and his distancing himself from it.

In any case, a week later, around 120 German priests convened the *Liebe Gewinn* or "Love Wins" initiative, inviting partners who lived together in non-marital unions, including homosexuals, to receive a blessing in their parishes or chapels. During the ceremonies, women preached from the pulpits, which is also forbidden by Catholic Church discipline.

At the same time, 230 German-speaking theologians signed a protest written by a working group from the University of Münster against the Congregation's *Responsum*, stating: "We believe that the life and love of same-sex couples are not worth less before God than the life and love of any other couple."[162]

---

160. See Congregation for the Doctrine of the Faith, "Responsum."

161. Gerard O'Connell, "Vatican Sources Suspect Pope Francis Was Distancing Himself From CDF Statement on Same-Sex Unions in Address," *America*, Mar. 21, 2021, https://www.americamagazine.org/faith/2021/03/21/pope-francis-same-sex-unions-statement-240291.

162. "More Than 230 German Theologians Protest Vatican Statement Against Blessings

Two priests from Würzbug collected more than 2,000 signatures of support from their parishioners.

Many churches in Germany flew rainbow flags from their bell towers or porticoes in protest at the Holy See's stance. The following year, the *Liebe Gewinn* initiative was held again in May in more than a hundred Catholic churches in Germany, including Magdeburg cathedral. In Essen, Auxiliary Bishop Ludger Schepers took part in the event in the church market, the first time a Catholic bishop publicly blessed homosexual partners.[163]

Turning a deaf ear to this official *Responsum*, which Pope Francis begrudgingly approved at the beginning of 2022, the diocese of Liège, in French-speaking Belgium, published a brochure titled "Welcoming, Accompanying, Carrying in Prayer the Life Project Shared by Homosexual Persons." It was presented to Pope Francis in July of that year. Two months later, the Flemish-speaking bishops, led by Cardinal Jozef De Kesel, then-president of the Belgian Bishops' Conference, published a three-page document titled "Being Pastorally Close to Homosexuals: For a Welcoming Church That Excludes No One." It stated, "This relationship, although not a Church marriage, can also be a source of peace and shared happiness for those involved." The text ends with a "Prayer for Love and Fidelity," which was widely received as a liturgy for the blessing of homosexual pairs.[164]

Cardinal Hollerich supported the Flemish bishops. When asked by Vatican Media, the Holy See's official portal, whether their

for Same-Sex Unions," *America*, Mar. 22, 2021, https://www.americamagazine.org /faith/2021/03/22/germany-theologians-same-sex-unions-blessing-vatican-240293.

163. See "Erster Bischof bei Segnung queerer Paare dabei," *Die Tagespost*, May 10, 2022, https://www.die-tagespost.de/kirche/aktuell/erster-bischof-bei-segnung-queerer-paare -dabei-art-228419.

164. "Belgian Bishops Publish Text for Same-Sex Blessings," *The Pillar*, Sept. 20, 2022, https://www.pillarcatholic.com/p/belgian-bishops-signal-approval-of-same-sex-blessings.

proposed liturgy could go ahead even after the Holy See's ban, he replied, "Frankly, the question doesn't seem decided to me."[165]

In March 2023, the German Synodal Way approved by a large majority a document titled "Blessing Ceremonies for Couples Who Love Each Other." Defying the Vatican, thirty-eight bishops voted in favor, only nine voted against, and eleven cowardly abstained.[166]

The most scandalous thing is that the main contribution to this favorable vote came from a speech by Bishop Johan Bonny. In it, he reported that during the last ad limina visit, the Flemish bishops presented Pope Francis with a text for a liturgical ceremony to bless partners in extramarital unions, including homosexual pairs. The prelate said, "The pope answered: 'It's your decision, I understand.' Twice he [the pope] asked, 'Do you all agree, are you all together on this?' We answered affirmatively."[167]

Concerned about this veritable tsunami pointing to a possible openness of the Church to such ceremonies and further aggravated by proposals put forward in the preparatory debates for the Synod on Synodality, five cardinals included among the dubia they presented to Pope Francis concerning the Synod on Synodality, a *dubium* asking, "Is it possible that in some circumstances, a pastor could bless unions between homosexual persons, thus suggesting that homosexual be-

---

165. "Relator do Sínodo da Sinodalidade defende uniões homossexuais e de divorciados em entrevista a site da Santa Sé," ACIDigital, Oct. 26, 2022, https://www.acidigital.com /noticia/53606/relator-do-sinodo-da-sinodalidade-defende-unioes-homossexuais-e-de -divorciados-em-entrevista-a-site-da-santa-se.

166. See Jonathan Liedl, "German Synodal Way Approves Same-Sex Blessings, Lay Preaching, and Reexamination of Priestly Celibacy," *Catholic News Agency*, Mar. 10, 2023, https:// www.catholicnewsagency.com/news/253842/german-synodal-way-approves-same-sex -blessings-lay-preaching-and-reexamination-of-priestly-celibacy.

167. "Belgique: le pape a accepté la bénédiction des couples de même sexes [MAJ]," LaPorteLatine.org, Mar. 23, 2023, https://laportelatine.org/actualite/belgique-le-pape-a -accepte-la-benediction-des-couples-de-meme-sexes.

havior as such would not be contrary to God's law and the person's journey toward God?"[168] The pope answered,

> The defense of objective truth is not the only expression of this charity. . . .
> Therefore, pastoral prudence must adequately discern whether there are forms of blessing requested by one or more persons that do not convey a mistaken concept of marriage.[169]

With these statements, the pontiff lifted a veil from what became, a few months later, the primary provision of *Fiducia supplicans*. Without fully accepting the proposals for formal liturgical ceremonies—which would mean changing the doctrine on sexual morality and marriage—Cardinal Fernández's document invents a *pastoral* extension of the concept of blessing that, contradictorily, would supposedly not imply approval of the sinful reality of the relationship being blessed.

Because of its ambiguity, this intermediate solution between the formal denial of Cardinal Ladaria's *Responsum* and the formal approval of homosexual relationships desired by the German-speaking bishops and the German Synodal Way is necessarily precarious. However, it paves the way for a change in doctrine, as the homosexual movement desires.

---

168. Luke Coppen, "Cardinals Ask Pope Francis to Answer Synod 'Dubia,'" *The Pillar*, Oct. 2, 2023, https://www.pillarcatholic.com/p/cardinals-ask-pope-francis-to-answer.

169. "Pope Francis Responds to Dubia Submitted by Five Cardinals, *Vatican News*, Oct. 2, 2023, https://www.vaticannews.va/en/pope/news/2023-10/pope-francis-responds-to-dubia-of-five-cardinals.html.

CHAPTER 11

The Final Goal: Changing the *Catechism of the Catholic Church*

As early as the 1970s, theologians, moralists, and pastoral workers involved in promoting the homosexual cause insisted there was only one way to eliminate the discrimination of which homosexuals were supposedly victims in the Catholic Church. It was to have her magisterium accept the "discovery" of modern science, especially after Sigmund Freud, that same-sex attraction and homosexual acts are not an abnormality but only a variant of human sexuality. The consequence of this necessary "updating" of Catholic doctrine would be to remove consensual homosexual acts between adults from the list of sins against the Sixth Commandment when performed within the context of a stable partnership.

After the condemnations from the Congregation of the Doctrine of the Faith against the authors promoting this doctrinal evolution—which naturally included a "re-reading" of biblical passages condemning such relationships as depraved—promoters of the homosexual agenda in the Church lowered their profile during the pontificates of Popes John Paul II and Benedict XVI. With the arrival of Pope Francis and his "Who am I to judge?" teaching, these demands have once again been proclaimed, first in a hushed voice and then from the rooftops.

An immediate obstacle is the teaching of the *Catechism of the Catholic Church* that same-sex attraction is "objectively disordered," and that "homosexual acts are intrinsically disordered" and qualified in Scripture as being "of grave depravity."[170]

---

170. *Catechism of the Catholic Church*, nos. 2357–2358.

Fr. James Martin is perhaps the most outspoken proponent of changing the *Catechism*. He presents its teachings as demeaning to people suffering from same-sex attraction. In his book *Building a Bridge*, Father Martin analyzes and criticizes the Catholic Church's attitude toward homosexual Catholics. As for calling same-sex attraction *disordered*, he writes, "The phrase relates to the orientation, not the person, but it is still needlessly hurtful. . . . So to call a person's sexuality 'objectively disordered' is to tell that person that all of his or her love . . . is disordered. That seems unnecessarily cruel."[171]

The American Jesuit animator of Outreach suggests changing the expression to *differently ordered*, which would imply—as canonist Fr. Gerald Murray rightly called out—"that God created two different orders of sexual behavior that are both good and right according to His will: Some people are homosexual by God's express design and some are heterosexual by God's express design."[172] If the inclination is simply different, and not disordered, then acting upon that inclination is simply different, and not disordered. Homosexual activity would be natural behavior for "differently ordered" people. Subtly, he insinuates that God intentionally created some people to be homosexuals. He tells homosexual Catholics to reflect on this question: "God, who creates only good things, made your 'inward parts.' How does that make you feel about yourself?"[173] And in a final prayer to God, the homosexual tells Him: "Jesus understands me and loves me with a special love, because of

---

171. James Martin, S.J., *Building a Bridge: How the Catholic Church and the LGBT Community Can Enter Into a Relationship of Respect, Compassion and Sensitivity* (San Francisco: HarperOne, 2017), 46–47.

172. Gerald E. Murray, "Father James Martin Proposes an Alternate Catechism," *National Catholic Register*, Jul. 10, 2017, https://www.ncregister.com/features/father-james-martin-proposes-an-alternate-catechism.

173. Martin, *Building a Bridge*, 113–14.

the way you [God] made me."[174] Therefore, any disapproval
of same-sex attraction and even homosexual activity would
be an attack on God's plan.

When asked by the Linz diocesan newspaper if the introduction of an official blessing would require a change in the
Catechism, Fr. Erwald Volgger, editor of the study on blessings
commissioned by the Austrian bishops, replied: "Of course,
because an official liturgy of the Church must have its foundation in Church doctrine. There is no other way." He adds, "The
Church's teaching is meeting with less and less resonance in
society and the Church, and moral theology in particular, is
advocating new approaches to the assessment of same-sex
relationships."[175]

Cardinal Jean-Claude Hollerich is another Church leader
who has called for a new assessment of homosexuality. A reporter from the German Catholic news agency KNA asked
him, "How do you get around the Church's teaching that homosexuality is a sin?" He answered:

> I believe that this is false. . . .
> So, I believe that the sociological-scientific foundation of
> this teaching is no longer correct, what one formerly con-
> demned was sodomy.[176]

In another interview with *Glas Koncila*, a Catholic Croatian
media outlet, the cardinal justified himself, saying, "When
Church teaching was made, the term homosexuality did not
even exist. Homosexuality is a new word; even in the time of
Saint Paul, people had no idea that there might be men and
women attracted to the same sex."

---

174. Martin, 146.

175. Wallner, "Mehr als ein normaler Segen."

176. Simon Caldwell, "Cardinal Hollerich: Church Teaching on Gay Sex Is 'False' and Can
Be Changed," *The Catholic Herald*, Feb. 3, 2022, https://catholicherald.co.uk/cardinal
-hollerich-church-teaching-on-gay-sex-is-false-and-can-be-changed/.

The journalist then asked, 'What about Paul's numerous rebukes of sodomy?" Without blinking, the cardinal retorted, "Sodomy was seen as something merely orgiastic at the time, typical of married people who entertained slaves for personal lust. But how can you condemn people who cannot love except the same sex? For some of them, it is possible to be chaste, but calling others to chastity seems like speaking Egyptian to them."

From the historical viewpoint, Cardinal Hollerich's statements about homosexuality in the Ancient World are baseless, particularly with regard to Greece, where pederasty was a social institution and whose pagan mythology included some homoerotic relations. Regardless of the historical record, writing to the Corinthians (see 1 Cor. 6:9 in the transliterated Septuagint), Saint Paul condemns the *arsenokoites* (man sleeping with man) and the *malakoi* (literally: "soft, silky, delicate"), i.e., both the active and the passive partners in a male homosexual relationship. He is not referring to a slave but to a consenting partner. More scandalous is the cardinal's claim that chastity is possible only for some. Does he believe in the power of God's grace? Based on this interview it would seem that he does not.

"Does that annul their calling to chastity?" the reporter insisted. The cardinal responded: "We can only charge people with moral conduct they can bear in their world. If we ask impossible things of them, we will put them off. If we say everything they do is intrinsically wrong, it is like saying their life has no value."

The journalist insisted: "Pardon our analogy, but is it not wrong to tell someone who inclines to steal not to steal too much? Should we not just say: 'You shall not steal'?" Cardinal Hollerich replied, "Yes, of course, we should. But a person with a tendency to steal can manage without stealing. A homosexual person will always love people of the same sex. We should not reduce homosexuality to inordinate sexual relations. That is a very crude way of understanding a human person."[177]

Once again, we ask, does the Jesuit archbishop of Luxembourg believe in God's grace? If, with supernatural help, a kleptomaniac "can manage without stealing," why can a same-sex attracted person not live chastely?

Other bishops' conferences have come to share this view that Catholic teaching on human sexuality needs to be updated. For example, some French bishops recently asked the pope to modify the *Catechism of the Catholic Church* to no longer condemn homosexual acts as "intrinsically disordered" and "contrary to Natural Law." The French Bishops' Conference has even appointed a commission of theologians to study the reformulation of doctrine on this issue.[178]

Once same-sex attraction is considered congenital and imposed by God on a person, and homosexual relationships in a stable partnership are considered not sinful, the way is open to recognizing the human group formed by the homosexual partners and any children previously born or legally adopted as a family. Hence, Pope Francis insists that civil unions of homosexual pairs be legally recognized.[179] However, that is not enough because to benefit from a "radical inclusion" into the life of the Church, progressive Catholics

---

177. Luka Tripalo, "Cardinal Jean-Claude Hollerich on Synodal Challenges, the 'Woman' Question, and the Disputes With Church's Teaching," Glas-Koncila.hr, Oct. 27, 2023, https://www.glas-koncila.hr/cardinal-jean-claude-hollerich-on-synodal-challenges-the-woman-question-and-the-disputes-with-churchs-teaching/.

178. See Marguerite de Lasa and Malo Tresca, "Homosexualité: Dans l'Église de France, des initiatives pour faire bouger le discours," *La Croix*, Mar. 3, 2023, https://www.la-croix.com/Religion/Homosexualite-lEglise-France-initiatives-faire-bouger-discours-2023-03-03-1201257664.

179. See Dominique Wolton, *Politique et société: Pape François, rencontres avec Dominique Wolton* (Paris: Ed. L'Observatoire, 2017), 321–22.

want to give homosexual pairs a theological status, even if not that of marriage proper.

An attempt at doctrinally recognizing such homosexual pairs as genuine families occurred during the first Synod on the Family in October 2014. To the surprise of the Synod Fathers, a section on welcoming homosexuals appeared in the *Relatio post disceptationem*, i.e., the report after debates. It was introduced by the Synod's special secretary, Archbishop Bruno Forte, without the topic having been widely discussed in the smaller language groups.[180]

The report asserted, "Homosexual people have gifts and qualities to offer the Christian community" since "there are cases where mutual support to the point of [self-]sacrifice is a valuable support for the partners' lives." And it wondered if the communities would be able to offer them a good welcome by "accepting and valuing their sexual orientation" (accompanied, of course, by this pious phrase) "without compromising Catholic doctrine on family and marriage."[181] These paragraphs were excluded from the final report and did not appear in the controversial post-synodal exhortation *Amoris laetitia*.

However, two statements had a significant impact in those months. The first was the interview that Most Rev. Johan Bonny, bishop of Antwerp, gave the Flemish newspaper *De Morgen*, in which he stated, "The substantive values are more important to me than the institutional question. Christian ethics assumes enduring relationships in which exclusivity, fidelity, and care for one another are central." He also affirmed,

---

180. See "Controversy Prompts Vatican to Clarify Synod Midterm," *Catholic News Agency*, Oct. 14, 2014, https://www.catholicnewsagency.com/news/30714/controversy -prompts-vatican-to-clarify-synod-midterm.

181. "'Relatio post disceptationem' del Relatore generale, Card. Péter Erdő" (Oct. 13, 2014), no. 50, Vatican.va, https://press.vatican.va/content/salastampa/it/bollettino /pubblico/2014/10/13/0751/03037.html.

"Within the Church, we need to seek a formal recognition of the relationship that is also present in many homosexual couples. Just as in society, there is a diversity of legal frameworks for partners, there must be diverse forms of recognition [in the Church]."[182]

The second position that drew repercussions was an interview with Cardinal Christoph Schönborn, archbishop of Vienna and one of the rapporteurs of the Synods on the Family, in the Jesuit magazine *Civiltà Cattolica*. In it, he reported that during the Synod, he insisted on the analogy that could be drawn between unmarried life partners and the Christian churches separated from Rome. Just as the latter have (according to the Second Vatican Council) elements of truth and holiness and tend toward Catholic unity, civil unions also contain positive aspects of commitment that are more significant than simple cohabitation, which brings them closer to a sacramental marriage. Therefore, the cardinal concluded, "We should look at the many situations of coexistence not only from the point of view of what is lacking but also from the point of view of what is already promised, what is already present."[183]

These overtures culminated in the official participation of these extramarital partnerships in the World Meeting of Families organized by the Dicastery for Laity, Family, and Life in Ireland in 2018, shortly after that country approved the misnamed equal marriage in a referendum. "While the Church upholds the ideal of marriage as a permanent commitment between a man and a woman, other unions exist

---

182. Remy Amkreutz and Koen Vidal, "Bonny wil kerkelijke erkenning holebi's," DeMorgen.be, Dec. 27, 2014, https://www.demorgen.be/nieuws/bonny-wil-kerkelijke -erkenning-holebi-s~b6075518/.

183. Antonio Spadaro, "Matrimonio e conversion pastorale: Intervista al cardinale Christoph Schönborn," *La Civiltà Cattolica*, Sept. 26, 2015, https://www.laciviltacattolica.it/articolo /matrimonio-e-conversione-pastorale-intervista-al-cardinale-christoph-schonborn/.

which provide mutual support to [couples]," said an official booklet titled "The Christian Vision for the Family." "Pope Francis encourages us never to exclude but to accompany these couples also with love, care and support."[184] In the original version, this text was printed above an image of two people embracing, one with a rainbow printed on his hand.

Whatever these Church-recognized homosexual unions are called and whatever the type of blessing employed to establish them, in the end, they will be perfectly comparable to a marriage between a man and a woman united by the sacrament.

According to Fr. Erwald Volgger, editor of the study on blessings commissioned by the Austrian hierarchy, the blessing that binds them will not be a sacrament but comparable to the religious profession or an abbot's installation. Here is a passage from the interview he gave to the press office of the Diocese of Linz:

Q: "What does the blessing of same-sex couples mean?"

A: "Volgger: A blessing is not a sacrament; it is not on the same level as the sacrament of marriage, but it is an official act of blessing the church calls a benediction—just like a religious profession, the installation of an abbot, an engagement ceremony, and the like. In concrete terms, this would mean that just as marriage between a man and a woman is an image of God's creative love, a same-sex relationship is also an image of God's care for people."

Further, he insists that if homosexual partners are faithful to each other, help each other with kindness and patience, and show benevolence, their relationship is an image of God's goodness. From a theological perspective, he adds that a

---

184. Michael J. O'Loughlin, "Global Meeting of Catholic Families in Dublin to Include Outreach to L.G.B.T. People," *America*, Oct. 20, 2017, https://www.americamagazine.org /faith/2017/10/20/global-meeting-catholic-families-dublin-include-outreach-lgbt-people.

blessing would have an official character that "expresses the church's commitment to the fidelity and exclusivity of the relationship."[185]

The core error in Father Volgger's main argument is that even in the worst sins a man can commit, there is always some relative good involved as the motivation for the evil action. Within the logic of his false premise, one could condone stealing since a thief's appropriation of others' property is often to ensure his future and that of his household, which is a reflection of Divine Providence.

Thus, the label given to these blessings is secondary because, according to the same Austrian theologian, God's grace is present in both the nuptial blessing and that of a homosexual union. That is what he says in another interview with the German portal *Katolisch.de*, which asks him if the ultimate goal is to equate the two: "When the Church's magisterium recognizes a same-sex relationship as a joint development of the baptismal vocation, it expresses that God is present and active in Jesus Christ. This constitutes the sacramental character of the relationship. Its name is not the primary goal. What is essential is the recognition of the shared way of life of two same-sex partners brought together by God. This theological dimension of grace is given too little consideration in the discussion."[186]

Swiss theologian Daniel Bogner goes further than his Austrian colleague. In an article for the portal *Katolisches.de*, he calls for a new understanding of what the Sacrament of Marriage means, freeing it from its "shell of perfection" so that extramarital, adulterous, and homosexual unions are not discriminated

---

185. Wallner, "Mehr als ein normaler Segen."

186. Christoph Paul Hartmann, "Volgger: Nicht nur Segen für homosexuelle Paare, sondern Anerkennung," Katholisch.de, Apr. 28, 2020, https://www.katholisch.de/artikel/25706 -volgger-nicht-nur-segen-fuer-homosexuelle-paare-sondern-anerkennung.

against by receiving a cheapened offer of blessing. According to him, those who ask the Church to recognize their union do not distinguish between a blessing and a sacrament. The Church makes a distinction because marriage is an image of the union of Christ with the Church, and of God's covenant with humanity, both of which are fruitful. Accordingly, "only the heterosexual union is considered 'marriageable.'" Those presenting themselves before the Church with a "love that is 'irregular'" are then confronted with the statement that "their union is in no way worthy of a sacrament, but that a blessing can be granted." Bogner sees this as discriminatory. To escape this dilemma, he proposes "to recalibrate the meaning of the sacrament itself, instead of using a subtle distinction between blessing and sacrament to narrow access to the sacrament in an elitist way and introduce a two-tier system of grace theology for life situations that cannot be addressed by the sacrament, according to the motto: sacrament for the few, blessing for a larger group."

According to Bogner, it is urgent to consider the demanding reality of lived partnerships because they are "a sign of a supra-worldly reality," which is the essence of sacraments. "The problem is that worldly realities are always flawed, finite and imperfect!" This is precisely the case with the institution of sacramental marriage. Its *formal* character requires the legally sealed, indissoluble form, but how this marriage is actually lived "is of no interest to church doctrine." For Bogner, man's imperfections should be incorporated into the understanding of the sacrament of marriage, "making the real life of the relationship much more of a criterion for the sacramentality of the marital union than has been the case up to now."

A renewed understanding of the Sacrament of Marriage should, therefore, according to Bogner, include the fact that marriages can break up. It could also "resolve the rigid fixation on biological sex and the necessary heterosexuality of the spouses" since "fertility does not have to be understood exclusively in terms of biological reproduction."

Given the above, and taking into account that the Church is a "field hospital," Bogner posits that "it is necessary to rethink the Sacrament of Marriage and free it from its shell of perfection" based on "the very real ways of loving between people," delivering it from "a tiered logic that distinguishes between a 'full form' sacrament and a cheapened offer of blessing for 'lower' forms of love."[187]

In other words, according to Bogner—who seems to be a good roadmap to understand what the homosexual movement hopes to achieve in the Church—in the name of man's "hardness of heart," one needs to reverse the restoration of marriage brought by Our Lord Jesus Christ's Redemption, as per the episode recounted by Saint Matthew (19:3–11), and degrade it to a level lower than that which prevailed in pagan society at the beginning of the Christian era.

---

187. Daniel Bogner, "Theologian: We Need a Marriage Sacrament for the 'Field Hospital,'" English.Katholisch.de, Feb. 12, 2024, https://english.katholisch.de/artikel /51022-theologian-we-need-a-marriage-sacrament-for-the-field-hospital.

CONCLUSION

In an interview with the Italian newspaper *La Stampa,* published on January 29, 2024, Pope Francis minimized the broad scope of the resistance to *Fiducia supplicans* by saying, "Those who protest vehemently belong to small ideological groups."

Unable to fit into this category the majority of the bishops' conferences of sub-Saharan Africa, which represent almost a quarter of the world's episcopate, the sovereign pontiff relativized their blunt resolutions banning blessings of homosexual partners with these words: "A special case are Africans: for them, homosexuality is something 'bad' from a cultural point of view, they don't tolerate it."

He concluded that he was not concerned about the risk of conservatives breaking away from the Catholic Church due to his reforms, saying that talk of a schism is always led by "small groups." "We must leave them to it and move on . . . and look forward," he said. "I trust that gradually everyone will be reassured by the spirit of the 'Fiducia Supplicans' declaration."[188]

After going through this book, the reader will understand that if there is a small ideological group with schismatic leanings, it is not to be found among the prelates, scholars, and faithful who defend the truth, goodness, and beauty of the Church's traditional teaching. Rather, it is in that small group of progressive dissidents that the Congregation for the Doctrine of the Faith condemned in the 1990s. Encouraged by Pope Francis's openings, it has raised its head and conquered space in the eleven years of his pontificate. Yet this homo-heretical current lacks popular support even in Germany,

---

188. "Pope Says Africans Are 'Special Case' When It Comes to LGBT Blessings," *Reuters,* Jan. 29, 2024, https://www.reuters.com/world/pope-says-africans-are-special-case-when-it-comes-lgbt-blessings-2024-01-29.

where it controls the bodies that direct the Synodal Way with the support of a massive majority of the hierarchy.

The reader will also understand that opposition to the homosexual movement (whose agenda will not be satisfied with a "pastoral" half-blessing nor rest until it obtains full recognition of "equal sacramental marriage") is not motivated by "homophobia" (a semantic weapon the homosexual movement deployed to denigrate and paralyze its opponents), nor any aesthetic-cultural preference. This is not about whether homosexuality is "ugly" culturally. Rather, it is because homosexuality is contrary to God's designs and a grave offense against the Sixth Commandment of His Law. Saint Paul is very clear about this in his Epistle to the Romans when referring to idolaters, those

> who worshipped and served the creature rather than the Creator. . . . For this cause, God delivered them up to shameful affections. For their women have changed the natural use into that use which is against nature. And, in like manner, the men also, leaving the natural use of the women, have burned in their lusts one toward another, men with men working that which is filthy, and receiving in themselves the recompense which was due to their error. And as they liked not to have God in their knowledge, God delivered them up to a reprobate sense to do those things which are not convenient (Rom 1:25–28).

The *Catechism of the Catholic Church* enshrines this teaching, which was echoed for twenty centuries by Church Fathers and Doctors, popes, bishops, great saints, and moral theologians.

Therefore, the doctrine condemning homosexuality is part of the Church's universal ordinary magisterium and, as such, is irreformable. Consequently, the notion that homosexual unions can have anything that deserves to be sanctified by a blessing—as *Fiducia supplicans* strives to impose on the Church's pastoral discipline—is unacceptable.

That is all the more so since this book's account makes it clear that pressure from the homosexual movement will not stop halfway but demand, as it already does, liturgical blessings with rituals similar to those of sacramental marriage.

Hence, Catholics must stand firm in an inflexible *non possumus* because "We ought to obey God, rather than men" (Acts 5:29). If this respectful but unwavering resistance to authority results in a split in the Church, it will not be the fault of those who defend the deposit of faith, striving to keep it intact, but rather those seeking to reinterpret it based on alleged developments of modern science and the supposed evolution of humanity.

As Plinio Corrêa de Oliveira stated thirty years ago, "Then there will be an internal clash within the Church, and this internal shock will produce one of the greatest upheavals in history."[189]

The higher the rank of Church dignitaries, the greater their responsibility in allowing any breach in the dam.

The prospect of this upheaval may seem daunting to the weak and those with little faith. But in the souls of those anchored in the Faith—confusing and painful as the horizon may appear—a voice from Heaven awakens a truly encouraging confidence: "Finally, my Immaculate Heart will triumph!"

Let us pray, therefore, confident in help from Providence and persevere in the fight. "Resist ye, strong in faith" (1 Pet. 5:9).

---

189. Roberto de Mattei, *Plinio Corrêa de Oliveira: Prophet of the Reign of Mary* (Boonville, N.Y.: Preserving Christian Publications, 2019), 224.

Works Cited

Abbott, Matt. "The 'Rainbow Sash Movement' Controversy," Catholic Online. Accessed Apr. 21, 2024. https://www.catholic.org/featured/headline.php?ID=2121&page=2.

Amkreutz, Remy and Koen Vidal. "Bonny wil kerkelijke erkenning holebi's." DeMorgen.be, Dec. 27, 2014. https://www.demorgen.be/nieuws/bonny-wil-kerkelijke-erkenning-holebi-s~b6075518/.

Bartmann, Bernhardt. *Précis de théologie dogmatique*. Mulhouse: Ed. Salvator, 1941.

Binnie, Isla. "Pope Accepts Disgraced Cardinal O'Brien's Resignation From Public Role." *Reuters*, Mar. 20, 2015. https://www.reuters.com/article/idUSKBN0MG20U/.

Bogner, Daniel. "Theologian: We Need a Marriage Sacrament for the 'Field Hospital.'" English.Katholisch.de, Feb. 12, 2024. https://english.katholisch.de/artikel/51022-theologian-we-need-a-marriage-sacrament-for-the-field-hospital.

Boorstein, Michelle. "D.C. Archdiocese: Denying Communion to Lesbian at Funeral Was Against 'Policy.'" *Washington Post*, Feb. 29, 2012. https://www.washingtonpost.com/local/dc-archdiocese-denying-communion-to-lesbian-at-funeral-was-against-policy/2012/02/28/gIQAlIxVgR_story.html.

Bos, David J. "'Equal Rites Before the Law': Religious Celebrations of Same-Sex Relationships in the Netherlands, 1960s–1990s." *Theology & Sexuality* 23, no. 3 (2017): 188–208. https://www.tandfonline.com/doi/full/10.1080/13558358.2017.1351123.

Caldwell, Simon. "Cardinal Hollerich: Church Teaching on Gay Sex Is 'False' and Can Be Changed." *The Catholic Herald*, Feb. 3, 2022. https://catholicherald.co.uk/cardinal-hollerich-church-teaching-on-gay-sex-is-false-and-can-be-changed/.

Cheng, Patrick S. *Radical Love: An Introduction to Queer Theology*. New York: Church Publishing, 2011.

Clark, J. Michael. *A Place to Start: Toward an Unapologetic Gay Liberation Theology*. Monument, Colo.: Monument Publishing, 1989.

Coday, Dennis. "A Cardinal Is Accused: The Groer Case." *National Catholic Reporter*, Apr. 4, 2014. https://www.ncronline.org/blogs/ncr-today/cardinal-accused-groer-case.

Congregation for Catholic Education. "Instruction Concerning the Criteria for the Discernment of Vocations With Regard to Persons With Homosexual Tendencies in View of Their Admission to the Seminary and to Holy Orders" (Nov. 4, 2005). Vatican.va. https://www.vatican.va/roman_curia/congregations/ccatheduc/documents/rc_con_ccatheduc_doc_20051104_istruzione_en.html.

Congregation for the Doctrine of the Faith. Declaration *Persona humana* (Dec. 29, 1975). https://www.vatican.va/roman_curia/congregations/cfaith /documents/rc_con_cfaith_doc_19751229_persona-humana_en.html.

———. "Letter to Archbishop John R. Quinn, President of the National Conference of Catholic Bishops in the U.S.A." (Jul. 13, 1979). Vatican.va. https://www.vatican.va/roman_curia/congregations/cfaith/documents /rc_con_cfaith_doc_19790713_mons-quinn_en.html.

———. "Letter to Father Charles Curran" (Jul. 25, 1986). Vatican.va. https:// www.vatican.va/roman_curia/congregations/cfaith/documents/rc _con_cfaith_doc_19860725_carlo-curran_en.html.

———. "Letter to the Bishops of the Catholic Church on the Pastoral Care of Homosexual Persons" (Oct. 1, 1986). Vatican.va. https://www.vatican.va /roman_curia/congregations/cfaith/documents/rc_con_cfaith _doc_19861001_homosexual-persons_en.html.

———. "Note on the Book by Fr. André Guindon, O.M.I. 'The Sexual Creators, an Ethical Proposal for Concerned Christians" (Jan. 31, 1992). Vatican.va. https://www.vatican.va/roman_curia/congregations/cfaith/documents /rc_con_cfaith_doc_19920131_book-guindon_en.html.

———. "Notification Regarding Certain Writings of Fr. Marciano Vidal, C.Ss.R." (Feb. 22, 2001). Vatican.va. https://www.vatican.va/roman_curia/congregations /cfaith/documents/rc_con_cfaith_doc_20010515_vidal_po.html.

———. "Notification Regarding Sister Jeannine Gramick, SSND, and Father Robert Nugent, SDS (May 31, 1999). Vatican.va. https://www.vatican.va /roman_curia/congregations/cfaith/documents/rc_con_cfaith _doc_19990531_gramick-nugent-notification_en.html

———. "Responsum della Congregazione per la Dottrina della Fede ad un dubium circa la benedizione delle unioni di persone dello stesso sesso," Vatican.va, Mar. 15, 2021, https://press.vatican.va/content/salastampa /it/bollettino/pubblico/2021/03/15/0157/00330.html#ing.

Congregation for Divine Worship and the Discipline of the Sacraments. "Negativa a la ordenación de homosexuales al sacerdocio" (May 16, 2002). Corazones.org. Accessed Apr. 22, 2024. https://www.corazones.org /sacramentos/orden_sac/homosexualidad_ordenacion_2005.htm.

Comstock, Gary David. *Gay Theology Without Apology*. Cleveland, Oh.: The Pilgrim Press, 1993. Accessed Apr. 24, 2024. https://archive.org/details /gaytheologywitho0000coms/page/n7/mode/2up.

Coppen, Luke. "Cardinals Ask Pope Francis to Answer Synod 'Dubia.'" *The Pillar*, Oct. 2, 2023. https://www.pillarcatholic.com/p/cardinals-ask-pope -francis-to-answer.

———. "Luxembourg Synod Calls for 'Gay Marriage.'" *The Catholic Thing*, Jul. 28, 2022. https://www.thecatholicthing.org/2022/07/28/luxembourg -synod-calls-for-gay-marriage/.

Curran, Charles E. *Catholic Moral Theology in Dialogue*. Notre Dame, Ind.: Fides Publishers, Inc., 1972. Accessed Apr. 24, 2024. https://archive.org /details/catholicmoralthe0000curr_c4f9/mode/2up.

———. "Homosexuality and Moral Theology: Methodological and Substantive Considerations." *The Thomist: A Speculative Quarterly Review* 35, no. 3 (Jul. 1971): 447–81.

Darnton, John. "Gay Issue Roils the Church of England." *The New York Times*, Mar. 19, 1995. https://www.nytimes.com/1995/03/19/world/gay-issue -roils-church-of-england.html.

DeBernardo, Francis. "New Ways Ministry's LGBT Catholic Pilgrims Get VIP Seats at Papal Audience." New Ways Ministry, Feb. 19, 2015. https:// www.newwaysministry.org/2015/02/19/new-ways-ministrys-lgbt-catholic -pilgrims-get-vip-seats-at-papal-audience/.

de Lasa, Marguerite and Malo Tresca. "Homosexualité: Dans l'Église de France, des initiatives pour faire bouger le discours." *La Croix*, Mar. 3, 2023. https://www.la-croix.com/Religion/Homosexualite-lEglise-France -initiatives-faire-bouger-discours-2023-03-03-1201257664.

de Mattei, Roberto. *Plinio Corrêa de Oliveira: Prophet of the Reign of Mary*. Boonville, N.Y.: Preserving Christian Publications, 2019.

Der Synodale Weg. *Handlungstext: Lehramtliche Neubewertung von Homosexualität*. Accessed Apr. 21, 2024. https://www.synodalerweg.de /fileadmin/Synodalerweg/Dokumente_Reden_Beitraege/beschluesse -broschueren/SW8-Handlungstext_LehramtlicheNeubewertungvon Homosexualitaet_2022.pdf.

Desmond, Joan Frawley. "Father Timothy Radcliffe's Designation as Synod on Synodality's Retreat Master Stirs Anxiety." *National Catholic Register*, Jan. 27, 2023. https://www.ncregister.com/news/father-timothy-radcliffe -s-designation-as-synod-on-synodality-s-retreat-master-stirs-anxiety.

Dicastery for the Doctrine of the Faith. Declaration *Fiducia supplicans* on the Pastoral Meaning of Blessings (Dec. 18, 2023). Vatican.va. https:// www.vatican.va/roman_curia/congregations/cfaith/documents/rc _ddf_doc_20231218_fiducia-supplicans_en.html.

Drescher, Jack. "An Interview with Robert L. Spitzer, MD." *Journal of Gay & Lesbian Psychotherapy* 7, no. 3 (Feb. 2003): 97–110. Accessed Apr. 18, 2024. https://www.researchgate.net/profile/Jack-Drescher/publication /244889348_An_interview_with_Robert_L_Spitzer_MD/links/5413bc 2f0cf2bb7347db270f/An-interview-with-Robert-L-Spitzer-MD.pdf.

Esteban, Carlos. "Obispo alemán espera que Roma deje de considerar la sodomía como pecado grave." Infovaticana.com, Jan. 10, 2024. https:// infovaticana.com/2024/01/10/obispo-aleman-espera-que-roma-deje -de-considerar-la-sodomia-como-pecado-grave/.

Flynn, Colm. "Synod on Synodality Report." EWTN News Nightly, Oct. 19, 2023. https://www.ewtnvatican.com/articles/synod-on-synodality-report-1711.

Fraga, Brian. "In Synod Reports, US Catholics Call for Women's Leadership, LGBTQ Welcoming." *National Catholic Reporter*, Aug. 16, 2022. https://www.ncronline.org/news/synod-reports-us-catholics-call-womens-leadership-lgbtq-welcoming.

———. "Pope Francis Thanks New Ways Ministry in Recent Correspondence." *National Catholic Reporter*, Dec. 8, 2021. https://www.ncronline.org/news/people/pope-francis-thanks-new-ways-ministry-recent-correspondence.

Francis, Pope. "Apostolic Journey of His Holiness Pope Francis to Georgia and Azerbaijan (30 September – 2 October 2016)—In-Flight Press Conference of His Holiness Pope Francis From Azerbaijan to Rome—Papal Flight, Sunday, Oct. 2, 2016." Vatican.va. http://w2.vatican.va/content/francesco/pt/speeches/2016/october/documents/papa-francesco_20161002_georgia-azerbaijan-conferenza-stampa.html.

———. "Apostolic Journey to Rio de Janeiro on the Occasion of the XXVIII World Youth Day—Press Conference of Pope Francis During the Return Flight—Papal Flight, Sunday, July 28, 2013." Vatican.va. https://www.vatican.va/content/francesco/en/speeches/2013/july/documents/papa-francesco_20130728_gmg-conferenza-stampa.html.

Glatz, Carol. "Pope Names 13 Consultors to Vatican Secretariat for Communications." *Catholic News Service*, Apr. 12, 2017. https://www.ncronline.org/pope-names-13-consultors-vatican-secretariat-communications.

Goss, Robert E. *Take Back the Word: A Queer Reading of the Bible*. Boston: The Pilgrim Press, 2000.

Guindon, André. *The Sexual Language: An Essay in Moral Theology*. Ottawa: The University of Ottawa Press, 1977. Accessed Apr. 24, 2024. https://archive.org/details/sexuallanguagees0000guin/mode/2up.

Grindley, Lucas. "The Advocate's Person of the Year: Pope Francis." *The Advocate*, Dec. 16, 2013. https://www.advocate.com/year-review/2013/12/16/advocates-person-year-pope-francis.

Hanigan, James P. Review of *A Challenge to Love: Gay and Lesbian Catholics in the Church*, ed. Robert Nugent, *Horizons* 11, no. 1 (1984): 203–204. https://doi.org/10.1017/S0360966900033508203-204.

Hartmann, Christoph Paul. "Ist ein Segen für homosexuelle Paare möglich?" Katholisch.de, Aug. 29, 2019. https://www.katholisch.de/artikel/22758-ist-ein-segen-fuer-homosexuelle-paare-moeglich.

———. "Volgger: Nicht nur Segen für homosexuelle Paare, sondern Anerkennung." Katholisch.de, Apr. 28, 2020. https://www.katholisch.de

/artikel/25706-volgger-nicht-nur-segen-fuer-homosexuelle-paare
-sondern-anerkennung.

Herrera, Arak. "Movilh cuestiona 'bendiciones' a parejas homosexuales: 'Es una nueva e intolerable forma de exclusión.'" T13.ch, Dec. 19, 2023. https://www.t13.cl/noticia/nacional/movilh-cuestiona-bendiciones -parejas-homosexuales-19-12-2023.

Holy See. *Catechism of the Catholic Church*, https://www.vatican.va/archive /ENG0015/__P85.HTM.

——. "Statement Regarding a Meeting of Pope Francis and Mrs. Kim Davis at the Nunciature in Washington, D.C. (Fr. F. Lombardi, Director of the Press Office of the Holy See), Oct. 2, 2015. Vatican.va. https://press.vatican.va /content/salastampa/it/bollettino/pubblico/2015/10/02/0749/01616.html.

Hume, Basil. "A Note on the Teaching of the Catholic Church Concerning Homosexuality" (Apr. 1997). New Ways Ministry. Accessed Apr. 22, 2024. https://www.newwaysministry.org/wp-content/uploads/2018/12 /Hume1997.pdf.

Jack, Jason Steidl. "Remembering Revolutionary Pax Nidorf, Who Founded LGBT Ministry DignityUSA." *National Catholic Reporter*, Apr. 11, 2023. https://www.ncronline.org/opinion/guest-voices/remembering -revolutionary-pax-nidorf-who-founded-lgbt-ministry-dignityusa.

Kirk, Marshall and Hunter Madsen. *After the Ball: How America Will Conquer Its Fear & Hatred of Gays in the '90s*. New York: Doubleday, 1989. Accessed Apr. 24, 2024. https://archive.org/details/marshall-kirk-hunter-madsen -after-the-ball-how-america-will-conquer-its-fear-hat.

Kosnik, Anthony, et al. *Human Sexuality: New Directions in American Catholic Thought*. New York: Paulist Press, 1977. Accessed Apr. 24, 2024. https:// archive.org/details/humansexualityne00kosn.

Liedl, Jonathan. "German Synodal Way Approves Same-Sex Blessings, Lay Preaching, and Reexamination of Priestly Celibacy." *Catholic News Agency*, Mar. 10, 2023. https://www.catholicnewsagency.com/news/253842 /german-synodal-way-approves-same-sex-blessings-lay-preaching -and-reexamination-of-priestly-celibacy.

LifeSiteNews Europe. "Cdl. Müller Speaks Out in Defense of Polish Priest Sued by Germany for 'Hate Speech.'" LifeSiteNews.com, Aug. 19, 2021. https://www.lifesitenews.com/news/cdl-muller-speaks-out-in-defense -of-polish-priest-sued-by-germany-for-hate-speech/.

Loredo, Julio. "Homosexualidad y teología de la liberación," *Covadonga Informa* (Madrid, May 1990), 8–9. Accessed Apr. 24, 2024. https:// issuu.com/nestor87/docs/covadonga_informa_1986_1990. For the written proceedings of the conference, see Joaquín Ruiz-Gimenez, ed.,

Iglesia y derechos humanos: IX Congreso de teología (Madrid: Evangelio y Liberación, 1989).

Magister, Sandro. "'Fiducia supplicans'. Le cardinal Sarah: 'On s'oppose à une hérésie qui mine gravement l'Église.'" Diakonos.be, Jan. 8, 2024. https://www.diakonos.be/fiducia-supplicans-le-cardinal-sarah-on-soppose-a-une-heresie-qui-mine-gravement-leglise/.

Mahler, Thomas. "Exclusif: 'Sodoma', le livre-choc sur l'homosexualité au Vatican. *Lepoint.fr*, Feb. 13, 2019. https://www.lepoint.fr/societe/exclusif-sodoma-le-livre-choc-sur-l-homosexualite-au-vatican-13-02-2019-2293213_23.php.

Martin, S.J., James. "A Mini-Interview With the Holy Father." Outreach.faith, May 9, 2022. https://outreach.faith/2022/05/pope-francis-speaks-to-lgbtq-catholics/.

———. *Building a Bridge: How the Catholic Church and the LGBT Community Can Enter into a Relationship of Respect, Compassion and Sensitivity.* San Francisco: HarperOne, 2017.

McDermott, Jim. "Interview: Sister Jeannine Gramick on Being Censured by the Vatican, 50 Years of Ministry and Her Hopes for LGBT Catholics." *America*, Jan. 7, 2022. https://www.americamagazine.org/faith/2022/01/07/sister-jeanine-gramick-new-ways-ministry-242155.

———. "Pope Francis Praises Sister Jeannine Gramick's 50 Years of L.G.B.T. Ministry in Handwritten Letter." *America*, Jan. 7, 2022. https://www.americamagazine.org/faith/2022/01/07/sister-jeanine-gramick-letter-pope-francis-242157.

McElroy, Robert W. "Cardinal McElroy on 'Radical Inclusion' for L.G.B.T. People, Women and Others in the Catholic Church." *America*, Jan. 24, 2023. https://www.americamagazine.org/faith/2023/01/24/mcelroy-synodality-inclusion-244587.

McNeill, John J. *The Church and the Homosexual.* Third edition. Boston: Beacon Press, 1988. Accessed Apr. 18, 2024. https://archive.org/details/churchhomosexual00mcne/page/200/mode/2up.

———. *Scommettere su Dio, teologia della liberazione omosessuale.* Casale Monferrato: Edizioni Sonda, 1994.

Montagna, Diane. "Archbishop Prohibits Priests From 'Performing any Form of Blessing' of Same-Sex Couples in Response to New Vatican Declaration." *Catholic Herald*, Dec. 19, 2023. https://catholicherald.co.uk/archbishop-prohibits-priests-from-performing-any-form-of-blessing-of-same-sex-couples-in-response-to-new-vatican-declaration/.

Müller, Gerhard Ludwig. "The Only Blessing of Mother Church Is the Truth That Will Set Us Free—Note on the Declaration *Fiducia supplicans*," in "Müller–'Fiducia Supplicans' Is 'Self-Contradictory.'" *The Pillar*, Dec. 21, 2023. https://www.pillarcatholic.com/p/muller-fiducia-supplicans-is-self.

Murray, Gerald E. "Father James Martin Proposes an Alternate Catechism." *National Catholic Register,* Jul. 10, 2017. https://www.ncregister.com /features/father-james-martin-proposes-an-alternate-catechism.

Mutsaerts, Rob. "Alweer die duivelse ambiguïteit." Paarse Pepers, Dec. 21, 2023. https://vitaminexp.blogspot.com/2023/12/alweer-die-duivelse -ambiguiteit.html.

Naumann, Joseph F. "'Fiducia Supplicans' Does Not Change Perennial Church Teaching." *The Leaven,* Jan. 12, 2024. https://theleaven.org /fiducia-supplicans-does-not-change-perennial-church-teaching/.

Neuhaus, Richard John. "Primrose Paths," in "A Sense of Change Both Ominous and Promising." *First Things,* Aug. 1995. https://www.firstthings.com /article/1995/08/a-sense-of-change-both-ominous-and-promising.

Novus Ordo Watch. "Austrian Homo Activist Says 'Cardinal' Schonborn Blessed His Relationship." YouTube.com, Novus Ordo Watch channel, Sept. 19, 2018. Accessed Apr. 18, 2024. https://www.youtube.com/watch?v=oV-g8aR01Sg.

Nugent, Robert, Jeannine Gramick, and Thomas Oddo. *Homosexual Catholics: A New Primer for Discussion.* Washington, D.C.: Dignity, Inc., 1980.

O'Connell, Gerard. "Pope Francis Encourages Jesuit Father James Martin in His L.G.B.T. Ministry." *America,* Jun. 27, 2021. https://www.americamagazine.org /faith/2021/06/27/james-martin-lgbt-ministry-pope-francis-240938.

———. "Pope Francis Received Father James Martin in Private Audience for the Second Time." *America,* Nov. 1, 2022. https://www.americamagazine.org /faith/2022/11/11/james-martin-pope-francis-244131.

———. "Vatican Sources Suspect Pope Francis Was Distancing Himself From CDF Statement on Same-Sex Unions in Address." *America,* Mar. 21, 2021. https://www.americamagazine.org/faith/2021/03/21/pope-francis -same-sex-unions-statement-240291.

O'Loughlin, Michael J. "Global Meeting of Catholic Families in Dublin to Include Outreach to L.G.B.T. People." *America,* Oct. 20, 2017. https:// www.americamagazine.org/faith/2017/10/20/global-meeting-catholic -families-dublin-include-outreach-lgbt-people.

Outreach.faith. "Pope Francis Clarifies Comments on Homosexuality: 'One Must Consider the Circumstances.'" Outreach.faith, Jan. 27, 2023. https://outreach.faith/2023/01/pope-francis-clarifies-comments-on -homosexuality-one-must-consider-the-circumstances/.

———. "Pope Francis Sends Greetings to This Year's Outreach Conference for LGBT Catholics." Outreach.faith, Jun. 14, 2023. https://outreach.faith /2023/06/pope-francis-sends-greetings-to-this-years-outreach -conference-for-lgbtq-catholics/.

Outright. "Matuba Mahlatjie Talks to Newsroom Afrika About the Vatican's New Stance on Same-Sex Couples." Outright International, Dec. 19, 2023.

https://outrightinternational.org/news-article/matuba-mahlatjie-talks
-newsroom-afrika-about-vaticans-new-stance-same-sex-couples.

Paprocki, Thomas J. "Imagining a Heretical Cardinal." *First Things,* Feb. 28,
2023. https://www.firstthings.com/web-exclusives/2023/02/imagining
-a-heretical-cardinal.

Pilato, Claudia. "Dall'omosessualità alla pedofilia: sullo scivolo della
rivoluzione sessuale." *Tradizione Famiglia Proprietà* (Oct. 2013).
Accessed Apr. 24, 2024. https://issuu.com/tradizionefamigliaproprieta
/docs/tfpottobre2013.

Pongratz-Lippitt, Christa. "Cardinal Leads First-Ever AIDS Day Requiem in
Vienna Cathedral." *La Croix,* Dec. 4, 2017. https://international.la-croix.com
/news/culture/cardinal-leads-first-ever-aids-day-requiem-in-vienna
-cathedral/6492.

———. "New Book Charts Path to Same-Sex Benedictions." *The Tablet,* May
6, 2020. https://www.thetablet.co.uk/news/12869/new-book-charts
-path-to-same-sex-benedictions.

Pontifical Council for the Family. "The Truth and Meaning of Human
Sexuality—Guidelines for Education Within the Family" (Dec. 8, 1995).
Vatican.va. https://www.vatican.va/roman_curia/pontifical_councils/family
/documents/rc_pc_family_doc_08121995_human-sexuality_po.html.

Progetto Gionata. "Il teologo Mancuso e le prospettive teologiche sull'amore omosessuale e il suo esercizio mediante l'affettività." Progetto Gionata, Apr. 27, 2012.

Quaranta, Pasquale. "Chiesa e omosessualità, intervista a Vito Mancuso."
Liberstef.myblog.it, May 8, 2012.

Ratzinger, Joseph. "Full Text of Benedict XVI Essay: 'The Church and the
Scandal of Sexual Abuse.'" *Catholic News Agency,* Apr. 10, 2019. https://
www.catholicnewsagency.com/news/41013/full-text-of-benedict-xvi
-essay-the-church-and-the-scandal-of-sexual-abuse.

Rodriguez, Cecilia. "Pope Francis' Welcome to World's Only Openly
Gay Prime Minister Rekindles Vatican Controversy." *Forbes,* Apr. 9,
2017. https://www.forbes.com/sites/ceciliarodriguez/2017/04/09
/pope-franciss-welcome-to-worlds-only-openly-gay-prime-minister
-rekindles-vatican-controversy/#6cb67112a607.

Rozados Taboada, Manuel. "La Iglesia y la homosexualidad." *Revista Española
de Derecho Canonico* 35, no. 102 (1979): 531–83. https://summa.upsa.es
/high.raw?id=0000005260&name=00000001.original.pdf.

Sánchez Silva, Walter. "*Fiducia supplicans* 'no era un tema' para Navidad,
asegura Cardenal." ACI Prensa, Dec. 25, 2023. https://www.aciprensa.com
/noticias/102489/cardenal-sturla-declaracion-sobre-bendicion-de
-parejas-homosexuales-no-era-tema-de-navidad.

Scaramuzzi, Iacopo. "Pope Francis Has Met Regularly With Transgender Catholics at General Audiences." Translated by Massimo and Sarah Faggioli, and Griffin Leynick. Outreach.faith, Jan. 13, 2023. https://outreach.faith/2023/01/pope-francis-meets-regularly-with-transgender-catholics-at-general-audience/.

Serra, Cristiana de Assis. "'Viemos pra comungar': Estratégias de permanência na Igreja desenvolvidas por grupos de 'católicos LGBT' brasileiros e suas implicações." Master's thesis, Universidade do Estado do Rio de Janeiro, 2017. Accessed Apr. 21, 2024. https://www.diversidadesexual.com.br/wp-content/uploads/2013/04/Cat%C3%B3licos-LGBT-Cristiana-Serra.pdf.

Shine, Robert. "German and Flemish Bishops Warmly Welcome Vatican's Declaration on Blessings." New Ways Ministry, Jan. 9, 2024. https://www.newwaysministry.org/2024/01/09/german-and-flemish-bishops-warmly-welcome-vaticans-declaration-on-blessings/.

———. "Pope Francis Meets With LGBT Pilgrims as Sixth Anniversary of His Election Approaches." New Ways Ministry, Mar. 12, 2019. https://www.newwaysministry.org/2019/03/12/pope-francis-meets-with-lgbt-pilgrims-as-sixth-anniversary-of-his-election-approaches/.

———. "Pope Francis Receives Sr. Jeannine Gramick at Vatican." New Ways Ministry, Oct. 17, 2023. https://www.newwaysministry.org/2023/10/17/pope-francis-receives-sr-jeannine-gramick-at-vatican/.

———. "Pope Francis Writes to New Ways Ministry: 'Thank You for Your Neighborly Work.'" New Ways Ministry, Dec. 9, 2021. https://www.newwaysministry.org/2021/12/09/pope-francis-writes-to-new-ways-ministry-thank-you-for-your-neighborly-work/.

———. "Priest Blesses Same-Gender Couple's Engagement in Malta; Archbishop Remains Calm." New Ways Ministry, Apr. 15, 2015. https://www.newwaysministry.org/2015/04/15/priest-blesses-same-gender-couples-engagement-in-malta-archbishop-remains-calm/.

Solimeo, Luiz Sérgio. "The Homosexual Movement Scores a Win in the Fr. Guarnizo Affair—Who Caused the Scandal and Why?" TFP.org, Mar. 17, 2012. https://www.tfp.org/the-homosexual-movement-scores-a-win-in-the-fr-guarnizo-affair-who-caused-the-scandal-and-why/.

Soulforce. "What Is the Primary Goal of Soulforce?" Soulforce.org. Accessed Dec. 2023. www.soulforce.org/main/faq.shtml. Printed 2003 website documentation in TFP archives.

Spadaro, Antonio. "Matrimonio e conversion pastorale. Intervista al cardinale Christoph Schönborn." La Civiltà Cattolica, Sept. 26, 2015. https://www.laciviltacattolica.it/articolo/matrimonio-e-conversione-pastorale-intervista-al-cardinale-christoph-schonborn/.

Stanley, Alessandra. "Pope Declares His 'Bitterness' Over Gay Event. *The New York Times*, Jul. 10, 2000. https://www.nytimes.com/2000/07/10/world/pope-declares-his-bitterness-over-gay-event.html.

Synod, General Secretariat of the. "Enlarge the Space of Your Tent"—Working Document for the Continental Stage (Oct. 24, 2022). Synod.va. https://www.synod.va/content/dam/synod/common/phases/continental-stage/dcs/20221025-ENG-DTC-FINAL-OK.pdf.

———. "'Relatio post disceptationem' del Relatore generale, Card. Péter Erdő" (Oct. 13, 2014). Vatican.va. https://press.vatican.va/content/salastampa/it/bollettino/pubblico/2014/10/13/0751/03037.html.

———. "XVI Ordinary General Assembly of the Synod of Bishops for a Synodal Church: Communion, Participation, Mission—Instrumentum Laboris—For the First Session—(October 2023)" (Jun. 20, 2023). Vatican.va. https://press.vatican.va/content/salastampa/it/bollettino/pubblico/2023/06/20/0456/01015.html#en.

TFP Committee on American Issues. *Defending a Higher Law: Why We Must Resist Same-Sex "Marriage" and the Homosexual Movement*. Spring Grove, Penn.: The American Society for the Defense of Tradition, Family, and Property—TFP, 2004. Accessed Apr. 24, 2024. https://www.tfp.org/images/books/Defending_A_Higher_Law.pdf.

Tripalo, Luka. "Cardinal Jean-Claude Hollerich on Synodal Challenges, the 'Woman' Question, and the Disputes With Church's Teaching." Glas-Koncila.hr, Oct. 27, 2023. https://www.glas-koncila.hr/cardinal-jean-claude-hollerich-on-synodal-challenges-the-woman-question-and-the-disputes-with-churchs-teaching/.

van de Spijker, Herman. *Homotropía: Inclinación hacia el mismo sexo*. Madrid: Sociedad de Educación Atenas, 1976.

Varnell, Paul. "Defending Our Morality," (originally published in *Chicago Free Press*, Aug. 16, 2000). IGFCultureWatch.com. Accessed Apr. 18, 2024, https://igfculturewatch.com/2000/08/16/defending-our-morality/.

Vatican. See Holy See.

Villar, Julieta. "Obispo aclara cómo se realizó la bendición a dos personas homosexuales en Uruguay." ACI Prensa, Feb. 22, 2024. https://www.aciprensa.com/noticias/103286/uruguay-obispo-aclara-como-se-realizo-la-bendicion-de-carlos-perciavalle-y-su-pareja-gay.

Wallner, Josef. "Mehr als ein normaler Segen." Kirchenzeitung.at, Apr. 28, 2020. https://www.kirchenzeitung.at/site/themen/gesellschaftsoziales/mehr-als-ein-normaler-segen.

Weldon, Terence. "Rainbow Sash Movement." QueeringtheChurch .wordpress.com, Mar. 6, 2010. https://queeringthechurch.wordpress.com /2010/03/06/rainbow-sash-movement/.

Wikipedia contributors. "Conchita Wurst." Wikipedia, The Free Encyclopedia. Accessed Apr. 26, 2024. https://en.wikipedia.org/w/index.php?title =Conchita_Wurst&oldid=1219830117.

———. "Rainbow Sash Movement." Wikipedia, The Free Encyclopedia. Accessed Apr. 21, 2024. https://en.wikipedia.org/w/index.php?title =Rainbow_Sash_Movement&oldid=1160411803.

Winfield, Nicole. "The AP Interview: Pope Says Homosexuality Not a Crime." *Associated Press*, Jan. 25, 2023. https://apnews.com/article/pope-francis -gay-rights-ap-interview-1359756ae22f27f87c1d4d6b9c8ce212.

———. "Vatican Apologizes for Removing Catholic LGBT Advocacy Group From Synod Website." *America*, Dec. 13, 2021. https://www .americamagazine.org/politics-society/2021/12/13/vatican-new -ways-ministry-synod-242024.

———, and Trisha Thomas. "For This Group of Trans Women, the Pope and His Message of Inclusivity Are a Welcome Change." *Associated Press*, Nov. 19, 2023. https://apnews.com/article/vatican-transgender-lgbtq -b3d67868504ba701cce09da9ecc94de0.

Wolton, Dominique. *Politique et société: Pape François, rencontres avec Dominique Wolton*. Paris: Ed. L'Observatoire, 2017.

Zengarini, Lisa. "Pope to Jesuit Fr. Martin: 'Jesus Is Close to Everyone.'" *Vatican News*, Aug. 3, 2022. https://www.vaticannews.va/en/pope /news/2022-08/pope-to-father-martin-jesus-is-close-to-everyone.html.

Zenit staff. "Cardinal Schonborn's Intervention at Presentation of Amoris Laetitia." Zenit.org, Apr. 8, 2016. https://zenit.org/articles/cardinal -schonborns-intervention-at-presentation-of-amoris-laetitia/.

Zimbrão, Natalia. "Dioceses do Brasil divergem sobre autorização da Santa Sé a bênção a uniões do mesmo sexo." ACIDigital, Dec. 26, 2023. https:// www.acidigital.com/noticia/57001/dioceses-do-brasil-divergem-sobre -autorizacao-da-santa-se-a-bencao-a-unioes-do-mesmo-sexo.

ZdK. "Zwischen Lehre und Lebenswelt Brücken bauen—Familie und Kirche in der Welt von heute." ZdK.de. Accessed Apr. 19, 2024. https:// www.zdk.de/veroeffentlichungen/erklaerungen/detail/Zwischen-Lehre -und-Lebenswelt-Bruecken-bauen-Familie-und-Kirche-in-der-Welt -von-heute-225w/.